THE TRIED AND THE TRUE

NATIVE AMERICAN WOMEN CONFRONTING COLONIZATION

THE YOUNG OXFORD HISTORY OF WOMEN IN THE UNITED STATES

Nancy F. Cott, *General Editor*

THE TRIED AND THE TRUE

NATIVE AMERICAN WOMEN CONFRONTING COLONIZATION

John Demos

OXFORD UNIVERSITY PRESS

New York • Oxford

*To Zoe Demetracopoulou
and Andromache Despotes,
my wonderful aunts*

Oxford University Press
Oxford   New York
Athens   Auckland   Bangkok   Bombay
Calcutta   Cape Town   Dar es Salaam   Delhi
Florence   Hong Kong   Istanbul   Karachi
Kuala Lumpur   Madras   Madrid   Melbourne
Mexico City   Nairobi   Paris   Singapore
and associated companies in
Berlin   Ibadan

Library of Congress Cataloging-in-Publication Data

Demos, John.
The tried and the true : Native American women confronting colonization / John Demos.
p. cm. — (Young Oxford history of women in the United States; v. 1)
Includes bibliographical references and index.
ISBN 0-19-508142-0
ISBN 0-19-508830-1 (series)
1. Indian women—United States—History—Juvenile literature.
2. Indian women—United States—Social conditions—Juvenile literature.
3. Indian women—United States—Government relations—Juvenile literature.
[1. Indian women—History. 2. Indian women—Social conditions. 3. United States—Social conditions.]
I. Title. II. Series.
HQ1410.Y68   1994 vol. 1
[E98.W8]
973'.0497'0082—dc20
94-33526
CIP
AC

1 3 5 7 9 8 6 4 2
Printed in the United States of America on acid-free paper

Design: Leonard Levitsky
Layout: Nora Wertz
Picture Research: Lisa Kirchner, Laura Kreiss

On the Cover: This 1835 oil painting of an Ojibwa woman by George Catlin is entitled *Jú-ah-kis-gaw, Woman with her Child in a Cradle.*

Frontispiece: Puebloan women bake bread in an outdoor oven.

CONTENTS

INTRODUCTION

O ne of the prime movers of the women's rights movement in the 1800s, Matilda Joslyn Gage, who was a close associate of Elizabeth Cady Stanton, lived in upstate New York, where remaining members of the Six Nations of the Iroquois Confederacy also lived. Gage and several other white women active in promoting women's property and voting rights admired the position women occupied in traditional Native American societies and saw it as a model for change in the legal system of the United States. In Iroquois groups such as the Seneca and Onondaga, Gage stressed, descent was determined through the mother—that is, children became a part of their mother's household, not their father's. Instead of the male-headed nuclear family (and the father's right to be legal guardian of the children) usual in Protestant America, in the "longhouse" a maternal line of kin lived together. Among the Iroquois, both husbands and wives could end marriages they no longer felt attached to. Women's work was credited equally with men's, although it was different. Neither sex owned or earned more; in fact, private property as whites knew it was not acknowledged. And the Iroquois system of government incorporated advice from the "matrons" of the group, although it was led by male chiefs.

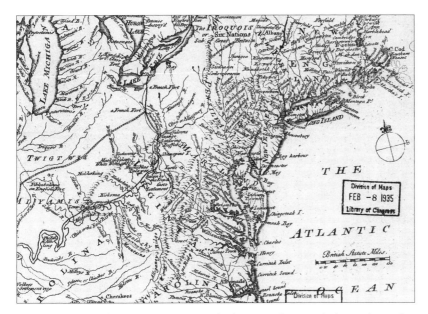

A 1754 map shows the location of the Six Nations tribes in New York and neighboring colonies. As white settlers moved west, Indians sometimes responded with violence, but more often they tried to cooperate with the newcomers in order to hold on to their land and traditions.

Yet in the common view of white (and overwhelmingly male) observers from the 16th through the 19th century, Native American women lived lives of drudgery, serving as "beasts of burden" while their men followed the sports of hunting and war. What was, in fact, the life experience of Iroquois and other major groups of Native American women? What was the social organization and culture they knew, and what did contact between cultures—between Native Americans and whites—mean to their ways of life? This book will map the outlines of their lives, their traditional societies, and the transformations in both caused by interactions with white settlers, missionaries, and the U.S. government.

This book is part of a series that covers the history of women in the United States from the 17th through the 20th century. Traditional historical writing has dealt almost entirely with men's lives because men have, until very recently, been the heads of state, the political officials, judges, ministers, and business leaders who have wielded the most visible and recorded power. But for several recent decades, new interest has arisen in social and cultural history, where common people are the actors who create trends and mark change as well as continuity. An outpouring of research and writing on women's history has been part of this trend to look at individuals and groups who have not held the reins of rule in their own hands but nonetheless participated in making history. The motive to ad-

This Hopi model of a pueblo is a children's toy. In Native American societies, as in white America, rearing children was primarily the responsibility of women.

dress and correct sexual inequality in society has also vitally influenced women's history, on the thinking that knowledge of the past is essential to creating justice for the future.

The histories in this series look at many aspects of women's lives. The books ask new questions about the course of American history. How did the type and size of families change, and what difference did that make in people's lives? What expectations for women differed from those for men, and how did such expectations change over the centuries? What roles did women play in the economy? What form did women's political participation take when they could not vote? And how did politics change when women did gain full citizenship? How did women work with other women who were like or unlike them, as well as with men, for social and political goals? What sex-specific constraints or opportunities did they face? The series aims to understand the diverse women who have peopled American history by investigating their work and leisure, family patterns, political activities, forms of organization, and outstanding accomplishments. Standard events of American history, from the settling of the continent to the American Revolution, the Civil War, industrialization, American entry onto the world stage, and world wars, are all here, too, but seen from the point of view of women's experiences. Together, the answers to new questions and the treatment of old ones from women's points of view make up a compelling narrative of four centuries of history in the United States.

—Nancy F. Cott

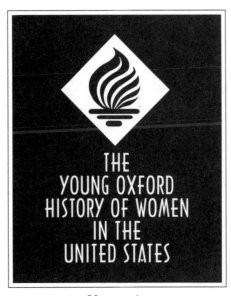

THE YOUNG OXFORD HISTORY OF WOMEN IN THE UNITED STATES

CHAPTER 1

INDIAN FOREMOTHERS AND THE COMING OF COLONIZATION

The first of the women we now call Native American were actually natives of Asia. They lived and died some 20,000 years ago. They belonged to small bands of prehistoric people who roamed the rugged wilderness of eastern Siberia and survived chiefly by hunting.

Today Asia is separated from North America by the Bering Strait, a waterway almost 40 miles wide. But 20,000 years ago (and in still earlier eras as well) the ocean was lower, and a land bridge rose between the two continents. Across the bridge, from time to time, moved animals of various ancient types—followed by the humans who hunted them.

From this remote beginning flowed the peopling of the Americas. The earth was locked in a bitter Ice Age, but between huge glaciers lay corridors of open land. The hunters and their descendants could walk these corridors from what is now Alaska to milder climes in the south.

The process was long and difficult, but by about the year 7000 B.C. there were people scattered throughout both continents. Archaeologists have found their traces—their tools, their graves, the bones of the animals they killed—in campsites as far down as the Strait of Magellan at South America's lowest tip.

Huron Indians as depicted by a French artist in the early 1600s. The two figures at the top are dressed for war, and the man at bottom right is ready for hunting in his fur-trimmed coat and snowshoes. An Indian woman and her child are shown at the bottom left.

Like other prehistoric groups around the world, these people lived in the manner of the Stone Age. They were nomads who wandered from place to place, in continuous pursuit of their game. The latter included mastodons and woolly mammoths (prehistoric elephantlike creatures), antelopes and wild horses, tapirs (distant relatives of the modern rhinoceros) and pigs.

Eventually, with the passage of many centuries, some of these species became extinct; perhaps the hunters had done their work too well. So they shifted their sights toward smaller game (deer and fox and other fur-bearers) and began also to develop new ways of sustaining themselves. Plant foods gathered in the forest became a major part of their diet: roots, berries, nuts, seeds, and fruit.

This change brought changes, too, in their social patterns. The human bands became somewhat larger and less nomadic. And the balance of duties between men and women gradually shifted. In the first period, men were the hunters and women their helpers. In

Mexican ceramic figures, dating from between 200 B.C. and A.D. 600, show women making tortillas from ground maize. Once Native American societies began farming, they settled into villages in which women often maintained the fields, harvested the crops, and prepared the food.

the second, men still hunted and women still helped, but women also took the lead in gathering the plant foods on which human survival increasingly depended.

More centuries passed, and their lifeways were further transformed. By around 5000 B.C. some Native Americans had begun the practice of farming; their crops included squashes, corn, peppers, and sunflowers. No longer reliant on the luck of the hunt or success in finding wild plants, these groups could build—and inhabit—settled villages. From villages grew still larger units, the seeds of tribes and nations.

These developments proceeded furthest and fastest in the region we know today as Central America. As long ago as 1000 B.C., a group called the Olmecs built an impressive empire in eastern Mexico; huge stone figures, which they carved into human shapes and apparently used in religious ceremonies, survive to the present.

The Olmecs were followed, in the march of history, by the Mayas, whose rule peaked between A.D. 200 and 600. Theirs was a civilization to rival any in Europe at the time. They lived in prosperous city-states, ranged across what is now southern Mexico and Guatemala. The cities were centers of both politics and religion. Their leaders were hereditary kings—and, at least occasionally, queens—who were thought to communicate with the gods. Priests conducted elaborate rites (including human sacrifice) in gracefully built, pyramidal temples. Gifted scholars created a sophisticated mathematical system and achieved the most accurate knowledge of astronomy the world had yet seen. Merchants traded between cities and ventured also to regions outside Mayan control. Beneath these fortunate classes labored a large mass of peasant-farmers. As with many Native American groups in later eras, corn was the key to their diet—and the focus of their everyday efforts.

By A.D. 1000 the Mayan cities were mostly in decline. Meanwhile, new empires—the Toltecs and the Aztecs—had formed in the so-called Valley of Mexico to the north. By this time, too, advanced cultures were appearing elsewhere in the Americas: for example, the Incas of modern-day Peru and the Mound Builders of the Ohio and Mississippi river valleys in the present-day United States. These, like the earlier kingdoms of Mexico, were agricultural peoples, but they also built cities and extensive networks of trade.

An illustration in the Florentine Codex, a 16th-century chronicle of Aztec customs, shows an Indian woman weaving, probably with fibers from maguey, cotton, or yucca plants.

Beginning in 1492, the lives of Native Americans were changed forever by the arrival of foreigners from Europe. Christopher Columbus was only the first in a long line of overseas explorers, and explorers were followed by traders, settlers, conquerors, and colonizers. It was, all in all, an invasion of massive proportions.

Columbus failed to realize, as he dropped anchor among the islands of the Caribbean, that he had reached a "New World" (new, of course, only from a European viewpoint); instead, he believed himself to be in the Asian regions known as the Indies. Thus he called the people who greeted him Indians, a mistake that has persisted to the present day. Had he known better—had he somehow gained the hindsight of our own time—he would have found these American groups to be almost as different from one another as they were from his own "tribe" of Europeans.

There were the peoples of the islands and of both the Atlantic and the Pacific coasts, fishermen (and women) whose lives expressed the rhythms of the sea. There were numerous tribes of hunters, especially in the upper half of North America, where the

The Great Serpent Mound in Ohio was built by an early Indian culture probably between A.D. 800 and 1300. Such earthen mounds were used as temples or tombs.

A 1590 engraving by the Belgian illustrator Théodore de Bry shows Virginia Indians making a boat (top) and dancing and praying. Men seem to be doing most of the activity here, but women's productive roles in Native American society were usually substantial; indeed, many European visitors thought that the women were overburdened with work.

environment allowed no other means of survival. There were the farmers of lower North America (our own Southeast and Southwest), of Mexico, and of the South American highlands. There were cultures linked to every conceivable environment: to mountains and prairies, and deserts and forests; to arctic cold and tropical heat.

Indian social and political systems ranged from highly centralized empires and sprawling confederacies to village-level chiefdoms and roving, family-style bands. Their ideas about men and women were no less varied. In some groups, women were leaders, in others, followers; in some, households formed around mothers, in others, around fathers; in some, women's work was central and primary, in others, it mainly involved assistance to men.

The languages the Indians spoke were too numerous for historians to count accurately; estimates range upwards of 2,000, not

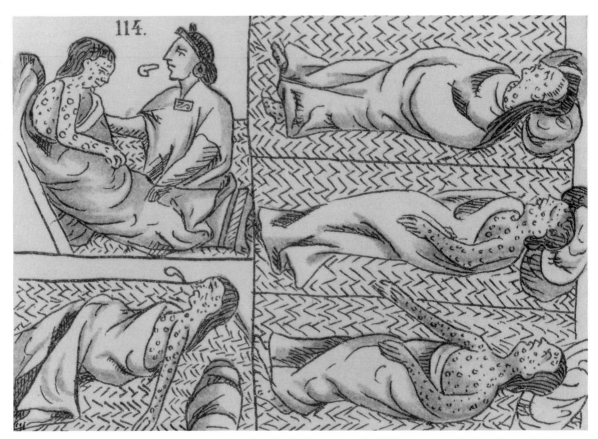

A scene from the Florentine Codex *shows Indians dying of smallpox. Native Americans had no immunity to this disease brought by Europeans, and epidemics swept across the continent.*

including local differences of dialect. Even their physical appearance was enormously varied. Some were very dark, others light-skinned; some were tall and rangy in stature, others short and heavyset; some clearly displayed the Asian features of their ancestors, others did not.

Yet to Columbus and to other Europeans who came in his wake, they were all of a piece—Indians. And they did share at least a few biological characteristics. To their great misfortune, for example, they were widely vulnerable to the unfamiliar diseases brought by the explorers and colonists from overseas.

Europeans had for centuries been attacked by smallpox, typhus, measles, and plague; huge numbers of people had sickened and died when overtaken by recurring epidemics. But Europeans had also, over many generations, developed immunities to these diseases; their bodies learned how to fight back. Native American bodies, by contrast, had no such capacity at the time when the explorers who carried the deadly germs first began to move among them.

The results were simply catastrophic; whole villages were wiped out in a single epidemic, and entire tribes disappeared within a decade. In some cases, such as the Incas of Peru, the European germs arrived ahead of the European people, having passed from one native group to another with lightning speed. The process began among the peoples of the Atlantic coast, but it was repeated with every newly exposed group. Epidemics moved in this way, steadily and relentlessly, from east to west to the very shores of the Pacific. Historians today can only guess at the numbers affected, but it seems that within a century of Columbus's arrival a native population of nearly 100 million in *all* the Americas had been reduced by at least half. In some particular regions the toll was higher still; in Mexico, for example, it approached 90 percent. And far to the north, among a tribe near the coast of New England, only a single man—the famed Squanto—survived to greet the first of the Pilgrim settlers.

These losses were not, moreover, entirely from disease. The Europeans did not shy from using violence—including enslavements, kidnappings, killings, and full-scale warfare, depending on the time and place. The Spanish conquistadors (conquerors) of the 16th century attacked and overwhelmed the Aztecs of Mexico, the Incas of Peru, and many lesser tribes as well. A hundred years later the English fought native warriors in the newly established colonies of Virginia, Connecticut, Massachusetts, and New York, while the French battled the Iroquois Confederacy along the borders of Canada.

But it would be wrong to describe warfare as the chief mode of contact between colonists and Indians. Virtually from the start, most natives reacted to most newcomers with something other than hostility: with open interest and curiosity, with mixed admiration and scorn, and with hope of gain for themselves. The newcomers seemed physically unappealing—they were too ruddy, with too much body and facial hair—while their social style was rough and undignified by native standards. On the other hand, their material possessions and technology were undeniably impressive: their large ocean-going ships, their finely woven textiles, their loud and deadly firearms.

The European newcomers, meanwhile, responded from the viewpoint of their own beliefs and values. To them Indians were "heathen," and thus prime candidates for conversion to Christianity. Indians were "savage," and thus in need of learning "civilized

In this 1598 engraving, Spaniards receive gifts from the Indians. Exchanges of gifts led rapidly into regular trade, and as a result, Native Americans became increasingly dependent on the goods brought by whites.

ways." Indians were "lascivious," and thus a source of sexual temptation. Indians were skilled at farming, hunting and surviving in the "wilderness," and thus could serve as guides for inexperienced colonists. Indians occupied land important to colonists, and thus must be removed elsewhere.

Each side wished, in the early stages, to use the other for its own benefit. Trade was perhaps the clearest example of this impulse: Indian foods, furs, skins, and tribally owned lands were traded for European cloth, guns, cookware, jewelry, and liquor. Inevitably, these exchanges were open to misunderstanding—or to outright abuse. Land was a particularly sore point. Usually, the colonists expected to obtain full privileges of ownership, while the Indians were offering rights of *use* only. In this, each side was following its own principles with respect to land. Still, in many other cases, their dealings seemed mutually satisfactory.

There also developed between the Europeans and the Indians a pattern of mutual learning, even of borrowing. Each side learned, to some extent, the languages of the other, and together created a "pidgin" speech in which elements of various tongues were joined. And each learned something of the other's cultural ways. Colonists embraced the flowery rhetoric and ritual of native diplomacy, while

 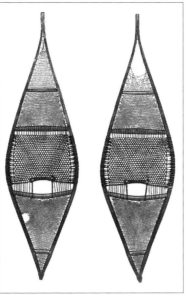

A Canadian wears snowshoes of Indian design; those at right were made by the Iroquois. Colonists frequently took advantage of Native American skills and crafts in order to survive in the new world.

Indians began to use European money. Colonists learned corn culti-vation from native farmers, while Indians grew grains, melons, and vegetables using seeds brought from Europe. Colonists used Indian-style canoes and snowshoes for travel; Indians raised and rode horses of European breed. Indeed, the list of such borrowings grew remarkably long.

To go through this list is to glimpse a process of two-way influence: natives and newcomers becoming progressively more alike. Yet the pattern would not last indefinitely. If the exchanges were roughly even at the start, they became increasingly *un*even with the passage of time.

Trade furnished many examples of the shifting balance. In the earliest years of settlement, the natives could frequently set the terms of trade: the times and places for meeting, the goods offered and received, even the rates of exchange. But after some decades it was the colonists who set the terms. Moreover, the eventual effect of such trade was to make Indians dependent on outside sources of supply; their clothing, their tools and weapons, even their foods were increasingly obtained from European sources. At the same time, and as part of the same process, native technologies that had previously supplied their needs were left to shrivel and die.

Warfare and diplomacy followed a similar track. At first, Indians would pull colonists into their own conflicts, as enemies or allies; but in the later colonial period, wars with Indians were just a limited part of larger European struggles. Meanwhile, treaty negotiations became a mask, or pretext, for removing native groups from the path of white settlement.

These changes reflected the increasingly uneven population numbers as both warfare and epidemics took a continuing toll on the natives. Each year there were more colonists and fewer Indians. Each year the pressure of advancing settlement increased. By the mid-1700s Indians were a rare sight in the coastal parts of eastern North America. And in the newly formed United States of the early 1800s, Indians began to be confined to what the government called reservations.

Nevertheless, Indian cultures—and Indian people—did not simply fade away. In fact, some of these cultures showed great strength in resisting and ultimately adjusting to the encroachments of the Europeans. The Iroquois Five Nations succeeded for more than a century in playing off the English and the French against each other while guarding their homeland in upstate New York. They succeeded, too, in controlling the fur trade between colonial merchants and native groups farther west: the furs would move through Iroquois hands and pay Iroquois tolls and tribute on the way to markets overseas.

Indians row toward Manhattan in the 1630s in order to trade their furs with Dutch colonists. This is the earliest known view of New Amsterdam, which later became New York City.

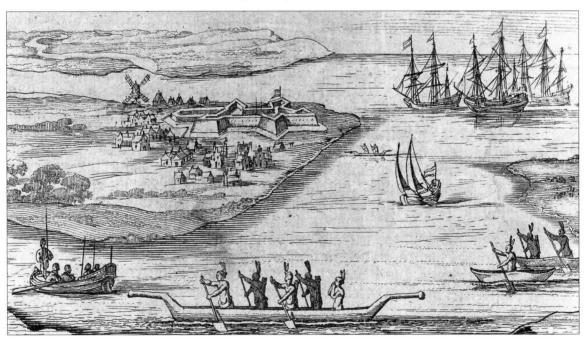

Farther south—indeed, all along the Atlantic seaboard—Indians pulled back and regrouped in order to save at least some of their traditional ways. A tribe that was decimated by disease or wars would join with others that had been similarly reduced to create a new group with added strength of numbers. Languages, religious beliefs, foods, and technologies were blended as a result—blended, but not lost. Moreover, the members of such groups would frequently find a means to enter the market system. Some continued their old pursuits of hunting and fishing, selling their catch to the highest bidder. Others worked as porters, laborers, or traders in their own right.

These developments were especially important near, or beyond, the frontier of white settlement. But the frontier was itself highly elastic—more nearly a region than a single line. Within that region appeared what one historian has called a "middle ground," in which white and Indian cultures were thoroughly mixed. Daniel Boone with his coonskin cap became a famous symbol of the middle ground, but there were equally clear (if less well known) symbols on the Indian side as well.

In many respects the Native Americans and the European colonists were more alike than different. On both sides the vast majority of people lived in villages and towns. On both sides, too, agriculture was the leading means of sustenance. European markets were more fully developed, but Indians were also quite familiar with trade. Europeans took great pride in their Judeo-Christian religious heritage, but Indians, too, maintained elaborate spiritual traditions. European medicines were more effective for certain kinds of illnesses, but Indian remedies seemed better for others. Europeans possessed important technological advantages—firearms were the most obvious example—but European visitors found much to admire in native basketry, leatherwork, and pottery.

On one point, however, Europeans found much that was different—and nothing whatsoever to admire. Indian cultures, they said almost in one voice, allowed—or even required—shocking mistreatment of women. At the heart of this criticism lay divergent patterns of work. In most of Europe, before modern times, farm work was primarily for men, while women labored in various home-based activities. In America, with the natives, the pattern seemed almost

Native craft traditions were much admired by early explorers and settlers from Europe. Shown here, from top, are Iroquois beaded moccasins, an Iroquois bark basket, and a Zuni bowl.

Women of a Great Lakes tribe scare birds out of the cornfields in this 1852 illustration by Henry Rowe Schoolcraft. Taking care of the crops, as well as the household, was often the women's job in Native American cultures.

opposite. There, in many tribes women took care of the fields: hoed, planted, tended, harvested. And there, too, women cut and hauled firewood, built and maintained housing, and did household chores besides. Men, meanwhile, were responsible for hunting and fishing—which Europeans wrote off as mere "sport"—and also for military defense. The gist was, as Europeans saw it, that Indian men exploited their women shamefully. The men seemed idle and lazy, while women were reduced to the level of slaves.

Such charges appear with striking regularity throughout the settlers' comments on Indians; no doubt they were widely believed. But a closer look at the settlers' actions suggests a more complicated picture. Consider the matter of Indian war captives. Many native groups, especially in North America, waged war in order to seize outsiders for adoption into their own families and communities. In time these captives came to include thousands of Europeans, chiefly French and English. Of the latter, most would eventually have the chance to return home, but some were so comfortable in their new surroundings that they chose to stay on. And among such "white Indians," as they were called, the largest number by far were women.

These facts raise a question: Why did so many female captives prefer to remain with their captors—especially if women's lot among the Indians was truly equivalent to slavery? Why were they

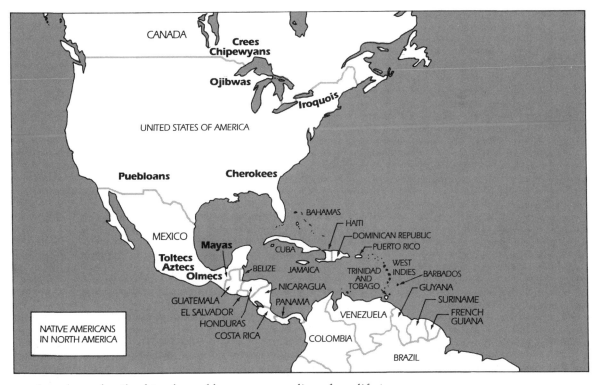

NATIVE AMERICANS
IN NORTH AMERICA

ready to leave family, friends, and home surroundings for a life (sup-posedly) at the mercy of "savage" men? Unfortunately, we cannot hear from most of them directly, but one famous "white Indian"—Mary Jemison, captured by the Iroquois in the 1740s—wrote in a published memoir about native women: "Their task is probably not harder than that of white women... and their cares certainly are not half as numerous, nor as great." Moreover, in her own case, Jemison had become "warmly attached [to her captors] in consideration of the favors, affection, and friendship with which they had uniformly treated me, from the time of my adoption."

Perhaps, then, there was more to the life of Indian women than what the settlers typically claimed. This book will focus on four particular groups: the Puebloans, of the present-day Southwest; the Iroquois, of the northeast woodlands; the fur-trading tribes (prin-cipally Ojibwas, Chipewyans, and Crees), near and above the Great Lakes; and the Cherokees, of the interior Southeast. Close views of different cultural settings will provide an overall sense of the possi-bilities open to Indian women—and of their gains and losses in confronting colonization.

CHAPTER 2

PUEBLOAN WOMEN AND THE CHILDREN OF THE SUN

A t some point in their long migration southward, the Native Americans reached the region of present-day New Mexico. Surviving traces of an Indian presence there go back at least to 9000 B.C.

What followed was the usual sequence of cultural change. As animal herds shrank, the original bands of hunters gradually became hunter-gatherers. By 2000 B.C. they had learned corn cultivation, probably through contact with farming communities farther south, and sometime after that they were growing squash and beans as well. They ceased to be nomads and built settled villages. They began also to produce colorful pottery and textiles.

By around A.D. 1000 their descendants had created a culture we now call the Anasazi. Its people lived in cliff houses high above the Rio Grande and adjacent river valleys. (Impressive remains can still be seen by modern vistors.) Because the climate had been slowly drying out for centuries, the Anasazi irrigated their cornfields with water from the rivers. Their villages grew in size; their farming became more productive. Their crafts were increasingly specialized and sophisticated.

In about the year 1500 a new factor entered the lives of these people. Groups of nomadic Indians from the north, ancestors of the present-day Apaches and Navajos, arrived in their vicinity.

A 1905 photo by Edward Curtis of Puebloan women filling jars with water. Curtis had by this time already embarked on a project to document the customs of the Indians of North America through photographs. By 1930, he had compiled 20 volumes of photos, with accompanying text.

Contact with the newcomers was sometimes friendly, sometimes not; there was trade, but also sporadic violence. Accordingly, life within the villages became more cautious and defensive than before.

The people of this region did not think of themselves as a single group. In fact, they represented at least a dozen different tribes (Hopi, Zuni, Tewa, Tano, Piro, and so on) and nearly as many separate languages. Nonetheless, they shared many beliefs and customs, and outsiders later called them all by the Spanish name for their villages, "pueblos."

Each pueblo—there were about 100 in all—managed its own governance. Each was led by "inside" and "outside" chiefs; the former were responsible for matters within the community, the latter for military defense. Spiritual concerns were pervasive; deities called "katsina" were thought to control the details of everyday life, especially the appearance (or absence) of life-giving rains. The katsina were worshiped in underground chapels called "kivas."

The village population was divided into large family groups called lineages. Older people ("seniors") and younger ones ("juniors") were linked together by complex bonds of social obligation.

The Taos Pueblo in New Mexico is a typical adobe structure of the Southwest. Rooms are built haphazardly on top of one another, doors are placed above ground level with ladders leading to them, and the village is surrounded by a low stone wall. Similar housing has been used by Puebloan people for many centuries.

The entrance to a Hopi kiva, or ceremonial chamber, is visible at right. The kivas had many functions among the different Pueblo cultures, but most importantly, they were used in religious rites. At left is Snake Rock, a sacred place where dancers offered prayers for rain to their snake-gods.

These bonds were expressed, as in many other native groups elsewhere, by elaborate ceremonies of gift exchange. Gifts were given and received for all important life events: birth, puberty, marriage, and death. The most successful citizens of the pueblos were those best able to confer such gifts. Some were thought to possess special powers as warriors, rain conjurors, and medicine men, further adding to their prestige.

However, the most important of all social differences was that between male and female. And the position of women was notably strong. Households were organized around senior women, who owned most family property and controlled its use. (A newly married man would typically move into his wife's family's house.) Women's responsibilities included, above all, the nurturance—the "feeding"—of others. Each day they ground corn, cut and dried meat, and prepared additional foods for family consumption—activities for which they were widely honored. Women also built and maintained housing and generally supervised family affairs. Men, meanwhile, tended the corn plots, conducted trade with outsiders (such as the Apaches and Navajos), invoked the katsina, and defended the community when it came under attack.

This pattern of mutual service was thought to represent the balance and harmony of the universe. The earth itself seemed to embody female qualities (the power of reproduction, for example), while the sky and the rain were male; from their union came the corn and other crops on which human life depended. These beliefs gave a sacred meaning to human sexuality; sex was seen to symbolize the cosmic balance. Religious ceremonies were sometimes concluded with ritual acts of sexual intercourse. And, just as women gave food to sustain the lives of others, so, too, they offered their bodies sexually—even to strangers—as a sign of welcome and alliance.

Weddings were events of great moment, featuring especially elaborate gifts. The families of both bride and groom were closely involved, and the ceremony expressed the different—but balanced—roles of each partner. According to Hernan Gallegos, a Spanish visitor in the late 16th century:

> Colored and ornamented blankets are set before the couple. The groom covers his bride with her blankets, and she places his on him, in such a way that they clothe one another... The people place before the bride a grindstone, an olla [a large earthenware

In her wedding outfit and white ceremonial moccasins, a new bride leaves the home of her mother-in-law. At right, a woman plasters her home around 1915. Puebloan women were responsible for plastering their dwellings, both inside and out, with adobe. Often, the interior was whitewashed for a finished look.

vessel], a flat earthenware pan, and drinking vessels. They also put a grinding stone in her hand... The gifts set before her signify that with them she is to grind and cook food for her husband... Before the groom are placed a bow, spear, warclub, and shield, which signify that he is to defend his home and protect his wife and children. They give him his crate and leather band for carrying burdens. Then they place a hoe in his hand to signify that he is to till and cultivate the soil and gather corn to support his wife and children.

Impressive as these rites were, it was not expected that marriage would last for life; most Pueblo people were wed several times. A man or woman whose affections changed was free to take a new spouse.

In sum, women's power was based on their place in the household, their control of property and of the earth's fertility, and their sexuality. Men, by contrast, predominated in local politics and in communication with the gods. Balanced though these roles apparently were, they also fostered a sense of competition. In ceremonies of childbirth, for example, women would mock the genitals of boy babies and praise those of girls. And men, for their part, would periodically segregate themselves to protect their energies from women's powerful demands.

In the spring of 1539 the people of the pueblos received a strange report: a "black katsina" was approaching from the west. Escorted by Indians of other tribes, and dressed in animal skins and gaudy jewelry, he called himself Estevanico and claimed extraordinary spiritual powers. At each stop on his way he erected large prayer sticks (crosses) and chanted unintelligible words.

Upon entering one of the Zuni pueblos, Estevanico was taken prisoner. Undaunted, he announced that other katsina—white ones, whom he called Children of the Sun—would soon arrive to rescue him. He demanded gifts of food and jewelry and access to local women—whereupon his captors executed him as a witch.

Estevanico's prophecy was fulfilled the next summer, when a large group of white katsina entered the pueblo country. Riding on huge monsters (horses), clad in glittering raiments (steel armor), and laden with fire-breathing weapons (guns), they did indeed appear to be Children of the Sun. Greatly alarmed, the villagers prepared to defend themselves. A short battle followed and the strange katsina triumphed completely. When people nearby heard the news,

Eagle dancers near Santa Fe, New Mexico, in 1931, perform a ritual ceremony. Among the Puebloans, communicating with the gods was largely a male responsibility.

This Spanish spur was found at the Pecos Pueblo, New Mexico, and dates from around 1600. Spanish colonizers demanded the Native Americans' property and labor and used their superior weapons to enforce their rule over the Puebloans.

they rushed to declare their submission by decking the conquerors' prayer sticks with ceremonial flowers and feathers.

Estevanico was, in fact, the black slave of Spanish explorers who had reached Florida some years earlier. And the white katsina who followed him were Spaniards from central Mexico. Their ambitions fired by rumors of "golden cities" in the north, they were attempting a new expedition of discovery. Their leader was a young officer named Francisco Vásquez de Coronado.

The result, however, was a bitter disappointment. No gold was found in the pueblos, and Coronado wrote later that his informants had "not told the truth in a single thing." He did not immediately give up hope, however, and he spent the following year exploring still farther north (in present-day Kansas). But in 1542, still disappointed, he and his men returned to Mexico to quell an Indian rebellion there.

The white katsina did not reappear for another 40 years, and life in the pueblos resumed its traditional pattern. But toward the end of the century a new phase began when Spanish Catholic friars (priests) took aim at New Mexico as a field for missionary work. Several preliminary expeditions, in the 1580s, gathered useful information on the natives. And in 1595 a newly appointed Spanish governor came to stay, accompanied by a modest contingent of soldiers, settlers, and priests. The governor's guns and horses overawed the Puebloans, and their chiefs swore allegiance to the Spanish king. The settlers built houses and chapels for Christian worship, and the priests began their work of "saving [Indian] souls."

From this point forward New Mexico was a colony of Spain; successive governors and other civil officials ruled in the name of a faraway king. The initial group of around 200 soldier-settlers in 1600 grew to nearly 3,000 a century later. Meanwhile, the native population shrank from perhaps 80,000 to 10,000 in roughly the same time period.

The colonizers prevailed—notwithstanding these numbers— because of their much superior weaponry. But the natives did not remain wholly compliant in the face of conquest. From time to time individual pueblos would resist and revolt; then soldiers, officials, and even the friars were liable to suffer capture or death. To be sure, retaliation for such acts was swift and sure; Spanish losses would be avenged tenfold or more among the Indians.

Apart from these spasms of violence, the pueblos endured a regular round of demands by the colonizers. There was tribute to pay—property, or labor, or both. (The Spanish name for this system was *encomienda.*) And there were demands also on the persons of the Indians, especially for sexual favors from the women. At first the natives responded willingly; in their minds the tribute could be seen as part of a gift exchange, and the sexual favors as a form of welcome. But receiving no suitable return, they would soon take a darker view.

However, the deepest pressure on their lives came not from the settlers and civil officials but rather from the priests. For these men, few as they were, planned a sweeping transformation of native culture. They began by attacking Pueblo religion. Indians were urged to renounce katsina "devils" and embrace the Christian God. In some villages priests would raid the sacred kiva, confiscate ceremonial objects, and erect crosses in their place. One bragged to his superiors of having seized and burned "more than a thousand idols of wood."

And this was only the beginning. In order to become model Christians, the natives would have to change all their customary ways and attitudes—their sexual attitudes, for example. What the Puebloans saw as a natural, life-affirming function (tinged, more-

The mission church at the Zía Pueblo in New Mexico was built around 1614; the portrait is of a Franciscan monk from the 16th century. In trying to convert Native Americans to Catholicism, Spanish priests often ridiculed the native gods, confiscated sacred objects, and tried to convince the Indians that their customs were "sins."

over, with social and sacred meanings) the friars called the "sins of the flesh." Individual sinners must, according to Catholic belief, be shamed, whipped, or otherwise cowed into repentance. And chastity, faithfulness between spouses, lifelong marriage, and physical modesty—ideas previously unknown to the Puebloans—must henceforth be embraced as supreme virtues.

The changes would extend also to the core of social organization. The priests aimed, for instance, to undermine the authority of seniors over juniors. Indeed, they presented themselves as the best and truest of "fathers," while urging younger Indians to reject their natural fathers. At the same time, they claimed a "mothering" role, offering gifts, care, and comfort to children. These efforts achieved some undeniable success. Young Puebloans would occasionally expose and incriminate seniors who continued their katsina worship in secret.

A katsina mask from the Zuni tribe. Such masks were worn by men, who portrayed the gods, during religious ceremonies.

A Hopi katsina doll stands in stark contrast to the image of Saint Michael found in a Zuni church established by missionaries. Although native religion was strikingly different from Catholicism, some priests worked to integrate the two—by comparing the katsina to Catholic saints, for example.

In all this the priests tried—again, with some success—to blend traditional Puebloan culture with parts of their own system. The prayer-sticks used in the katsina cults could be likened to Christian crosses. The katsina themselves could be compared to Catholic saints. The ancestral Corn Mother, another key figure in Pueblo religion, could be seen as an imperfect representation of the Virgin Mary. The magic of native medicine men could be matched, or exceeded, by the healing rites of the friars. Even rain conjuring could be reshaped as Christian prayer. Moreover, in exercising their various powers, the priests would seem to be acting like "inside chiefs," while the Spanish governor took on the role of "outside chief" and the soldiers, the role of young warriors.

Key parts of the friars' assault on native culture concerned the position of women. Their efforts to suppress exuberant—and sometimes generous—female sexuality increased as time went along. And these efforts were paralleled by their disapproval of women's fertility societies, groups devoted to venerating "mother earth."

To be sure, the friars mixed such elements of woman-suppression with gestures of apparent sympathy. When Indian women were exploited—sexually or otherwise—by Spanish settlers, it was the priests who came to their defense. Moreover, native women could find reward and solace in the Catholic adoration of Mary. So, too, could they win approval for assisting the mission churches in tasks such as baking communion bread and cleaning vestments (priests' ceremonial robes) and altar linens.

Yet, considered as a whole, Catholic Christianity was distinctly patriarchal, or man-centered, with God the Father, Christ the Son, and an entirely male priesthood. Hence the weight it pressed on Pueblo culture went largely against women. Historians have noticed a striking link: In those pueblos least affected by Christianity, families continued to be organized around mothers (a *matrilineal* principle), and some degree of fertility worship survived. In other pueblos where missionary influence was strong, matrilineal fam-

Unmarried Hopi girls in Arizona can be identified by their hair whorls. To the Puebloan culture, the strict Catholic codes that imposed chastity before marriage and prohibited divorce were new and strange concepts.

ilies gave way to patrilineal ones, and fertility rites of all kinds disappeared.

Of course, native women had dealings with many other Europeans besides the priests. And although these others also maintained patriarchal standards, their effect on the women was quite complex. What were the circumstances that brought the two groups—Spanish settlers and Puebloan women—together? And how much did they influence one another?

Most settlers in the original group, at least 90 percent, were men. This meant that they had to look to the Indians for female companionship. Some took Puebloan women into their houses (and beds) as mistresses. Others formalized such relationships with rites of marriage. Of course, there were many looser connections as well: casual, short-term sprees, or sex for money (prostitution), or forcible rapes. The variety was wide, but a common result was half-breed children: *mestizos,* in the Spanish. Eventually, this group would form a large part of the total New Mexican population.

Native women also played important work roles in relation to the colonists. Many Spaniards hired household maids from within the pueblos; their duties included cooking, cleaning, child care, and other domestic chores. A few served as interpreters. Indians were frequently in demand as seamstresses and weavers. Their blankets and other textiles proved important both for personal use and in trade. The same was true of the pine nuts and berries gathered by Indian women. Ironware, leatherwork, and some foodstuffs had to be imported from Mexico, and Indian-made articles were offered in exchange.

Puebloan women had for generations played a leading role in house building; many were expert plasterers. This custom seemed surprising, and inappropriate, to the early Spanish settlers, and some wished to change it. But the natives proved resistant. "If we compel any man to work on building a house," wrote one of the priests, "the women laugh at him... and he runs away." In fact, the shame of such incidents went so deep that some of the men involved would actually leave for good and take up with the nearby Apaches.

In time the colonists accepted the native pattern and sought to benefit from it. Women continued to work as builders, for Span-

Blankets, clothes, and other textiles produced by Puebloan women were often offered in trade with Europeans. Women traditionally used cotton for weaving but began using wool as well after the Spanish introduced sheep to the area.

iards as well as their own people. Indeed, in the 19th century, when visitors arrived from other parts of America, they too were amazed at the sight of women builders. But plastering has remained an important role for Indian women of the Southwest right up to the present day.

Other traditional work activities of the women also won appreciation from the colonists. As far back as the 1540s, a member of Coronado's expedition had noted their production of "earthenware... jars of extraordinary labor and workmanship." Their textiles were no less impressive, especially the delicate embroidery and painted design. Puebloan women owned, and tended, large flocks of turkeys (another surprise for the Spanish). In every case, the products might easily enter settler households and then become part of the larger colonial trade.

Significantly, too, the women adopted materials and methods from the colonists in order to diversify or improve on their own

Hopi women building a house in Arizona. Once the structure is up, they will then plaster the walls with adobe.

Zuni pottery was much admired by the Europeans. The bold patterns on these earthenware jars are a distinctive feature.

craftsmanship. Their textiles had traditionally been made from cotton, but when the Spanish introduced sheep to the Southwest, wool became an equally popular fiber. Moreover, the use of sheepskin fragments to set plaster made building easier and the final result stronger. And foods brought from Spain (peaches, melons, apricots) and Mexico (tomatoes and chilies) could be incorporated into their cooking, with important consequences for native diet.

All such developments modified, but did not obliterate, traditional native ways. And they may actually have worked to strengthen the position of Puebloan women. It is worth noting, too, that women in the neighboring tribes—for example, the Apaches and Navajos— modeled their own work roles on the Puebloans. They, too, would become potters and textile makers of great skill, and they, too, would eventually learn plastering.

The middle decades of the 17th century were a time of simmering discontent in the pueblos. There was repeated drought, leading to crop failure, leading to famine. Apache and Navajo neighbors, themselves on the brink of starvation, carried out frequent, deadly raids. The Spanish governors bickered continually with the priests, and, as often as not, the Indians were caught in the middle.

Finally, in the summer of 1680, after months of secret planning, the pueblos rose together in open revolt. Eight thousand war-

In 1905, Puebloan women harvest peaches, a fruit from Spain that the Indians incorporated into their diet, along with other European foods. The woman at left takes a break from the work to breast-feed her child.

riors (including some from their erstwhile enemies, the Apaches) swept into battle under the leadership of a Tewa medicine man named Popé. Within a few days Spanish settlements throughout New Mexico lay in ruins and hundreds of settlers, including dozens of friars, were dead. The following months brought a determined campaign to replace foreign with traditional Indian ways. Christianity, the Spanish language, European foods, clothing, and social customs— all must be destroyed without a trace.

But that could not—and did not—happen. Droughts continued. The Puebloans and the Apaches quarreled. And even inside the pueblos there was dissension—which in some cases amounted to civil war. The Spanish, for their part, would not accept defeat; after a decade of withdrawal, they began (from their bases to the south) the process of reconquering New Mexico. By 1692 they had succeeded.

But the result of reconquest was not simply to repeat earlier patterns. The priests, for one thing, would operate only in a much reduced role. The settlers and soldiers would, from now on, live in well-protected fortresslike communities. And the pueblos themselves, especially those at some distance from the Spanish, would try to maintain their own protected world. Insofar as possible they continued their ancient rites and other cultural practices in private (or, in the case of the kivas, literally underground).

The pueblos were not, however, entirely immune to outside pressure. The Spanish continued to demand tribute labor, and most pueblos, however reluctantly, complied. At stated times and places work gangs reported to Spanish officials for assignment—the men, typically, to dig irrigation ditches and cultivate the governor's fields, the women to perform domestic chores. In theory, no one was exempt, including (in the words of the law) "even pregnant women."

In fact, this system of draft labor posed special dangers to women, pregnant or not. Sexual abuse of draftees by Spanish men seems to have been commonplace. "When Indian women enter Santa Fe [the colonial capital] to mill wheat or spin wool," reported a local priest, "they return to their pueblos deflowered and crying over their dishonor." Worse still, some of these attacks themselves led to pregnancy, and often, when that happened, both the woman and her child were disowned by her family. Such persons (called by Spaniards *genizaros,* which means "mixed" or "hybrid") would then have no place to turn except the Spanish towns, where they might subsist as household domestics under conditions not far from slavery. For them, continued abuse, sexual and otherwise, was almost a certainty.

These were perhaps the worst of the human casualties of Spanish colonization. But they remained just a part of the larger story. Another part, no less important and affecting, involved the many Puebloan women who managed to accommodate the pressures of colonization—and even to shape the terms of that accom-

A Zuni war chief, photographed in 1873, holds a Spanish cane and a rifle. Puebloan people, like Native Americans elsewhere, readily incorporated European objects into their own lives and cultures.

modation. Their importance as mothers, as workers, and as guardians of cherished traditions would long outlast the rule of the colonizers.

Indeed, the Puebloans remain one of the most vibrant of all native societies in the present-day United States. They have responded very forcefully to modern economic conditions; they profit, for example, from tourism in and around their settlements. Yet they have kept their own identity, and their pride, as a people distinct from their Anglo neighbors.

To this process of development and change, women's role has always been central. Baskets, pottery, and textiles made by Puebloan women now earn widespread admiration—and money. Traditional skills, applied under altered conditions: this has been their strategy through many succeeding generations.

One specific case may stand for the rest. Near the end of the 19th century, fragments of ancient pottery began to appear in archaeological excavations near the Hopi pueblos of central Arizona. Their style and methods, long since forgotten, were then taken up

In 1926, tourists arrive at the Tesuque Pueblo in New Mexico. In accommodating to white society, the Puebloans have learned to profit from the tourist business while maintaining local culture and crafts.

The potter Nampeyo at work inside a pueblo in Arizona around 1911. Her use of traditional designs and methods sparked new interest in Puebloan ceramics, and Native American potters today continue to produce traditional pieces for tourists and collectors.

by a local craftswoman named Nampeyo. Her work in turn sparked a major resurgence of Puebloan ceramic traditions. Nampeyo's pots revived designs not seen in centuries; moreover, she extended the old forms to make new ones as well. Her work would henceforth be sold in shops, hotels, and railroad stations throughout the Southwest.

Nampeyo's achievement was a modern echo of a theme first sounded in the era of colonization—when Puebloan women saved the old by accommodating the new, and through it all *survived*.

CHAPTER 3

IROQUOIS WOMEN AND THE VILLAGE WORLD

Accoding to the people we now know as Iroquois, history began with a godlike being called Sky Woman. Pushed from her home in the heavens by her jealous, uncaring husband, she fell toward an endless lake below. But birds and ducks flew to break her fall, and a turtle emerged from the waters to provide a resting place. Animals brought earth to put on the turtle's back—which, with Sky Woman's help, grew into the continent of North America. Presently, Sky Woman bore a daughter, and the daughter in turn bore twin sons. One of them, the Good Twin, improved the land and brought human beings to life. His brother, the Evil Twin, tried to destroy these works of creation, and eventually the two fought. Fortunately, the Good Twin triumphed and began teaching humans how to farm, how to govern themselves, and how to communicate with the spirit world.

This origin myth cannot, of course, be taken literally; but it illustrates the importance of women to the Iroquois. Other Iroquois myths have a similar emphasis; they tell, for example, of long migrations throughout North America—frequently under the leadership of a woman.

The actual origins of the Iroquois are difficult to discover. They do seem, as their myths suggest, to have been migrants from elsewhere. Their most likely ancestors were a people called Owasco

This contemporary clay figure of a clan mother was sculpted by Tammy Tarbell of the Mohawk tribe. Iroquois matrons had great influence in their society and were perhaps the most powerful women in any Native American tribe.

who, by about A.D. 1000, were established to the south and east of the Great Lakes. The Owasco, like the Iroquois later on, lived in compact villages and supported themselves through hunting and farming. As the centuries passed, these communities fell into recurrent warfare, while trade and other forms of contact among them dwindled almost to nothing. Eventually, they came together to make a "Great Peace"—there are powerful legends about that as well—and entered a new phase of their history. The peace would thereafter be kept by a "League" of their "Five Nations": the Mohawk, the Oneida, the Onondaga, the Cayuga, and the Seneca. This group—to which a sixth, the Tuscarora, would be added in the 18th century—made up the famed Iroquois Confederacy.

For protective reasons Iroquois villages were set on hilltops and enclosed by high palisade fences. Each one contained a cluster of several dozen residential buildings called longhouses. These were large, tunnel-like structures framed by tree limbs and covered with huge strips of bark. On the land beside the palisades stretched farm fields, and beyond the fields rose the dark shapes of the forest. The Iroquois themselves spoke of the "village world" and the "forest world" as separate places with entirely different modes of life.

The village world was, first and foremost, a world of women. The local population was organized into large clans, and the clans

A typical Iroquois village contained a cluster of bark-covered longhouses. The best site for a village was on a hilltop, which made it easier to defend against enemy war parties.

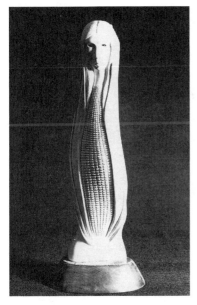

themselves were composed of families—with women at the center in each case. When young Iroquois married, they usually took up residence in the wife's longhouse; there they would join other members of her clan and family (mother, aunts, sisters, female cousins, and related menfolk). Their children were considered to belong to her family's "line" and would, when grown, inherit property from the same source. The husband, meanwhile, remained closely allied with his own mother's household; indeed, according to one account, "his mother and his sisters are more dear to him than his wife."

Women also bore a primary responsibility to *provide*—for themselves, for their children and other relatives, and for the community at large. The land belonged to them, not their husbands and brothers. So, too, did the crops, especially the so-called three sisters—corn, squash, and beans—on which human life was thought to depend. Work parties of women labored in the fields all through the summer season.

Corn cultivation was a particularly elaborate focus of activity. In addition to performing the basic tasks of planting, tending, and harvesting, women dried and braided the mature husks, shelled the kernels for storage, ground the stored kernels into flour, sifted the flour in preparation for cooking, and boiled the result into a variety of stews—all the while retaining a few bits for the *next* summer's planting. Every Iroquois girl learned the various steps at an early

The "three sisters"—corn, beans, and squash, staples of the traditional Iroquois diet— assume female forms in these sculptures by Stan Hill of the Mohawk tribe. All three are carved from moose antlers.

With their focus on home and village life, Iroquois women produced a variety of household objects for their family and community. At far right is a woven sash with a beaded design; to its left is a birchbark box decorated with quills.

age. And every Iroquois woman was honored for her part in this work, through a variety of seasonal festivals.

Moreover, women's responsibilities extended well beyond home care and farming. Berries, fruits, nuts, and other gathered products were also important to the Iroquois diet—and were also part of the female domain. Meat was obtained by men in far-ranging hunts, but women were much involved in skinning, packing, and otherwise preparing the animal carcasses for consumption. Women joined men in springtime fishing expeditions at strategic sites on nearby streams. Women were centrally involved in craft production: basketry, pottery, rope making, and leather work. Taken together, these activities secured their preeminence in the village world.

The men, for their part, were dominant in the forest world. And hunting was only a part of what they did there. Men led in dealings with outsiders—with fellow Iroquois from other villages and regions and with strangers from beyond Iroquois lands altogether. Men, therefore, were traders, diplomats, and above all, warriors. Yet precisely because these duties took them away for long periods, their position within the village was weakened.

Men did, to be sure, also decide matters of policy. Iroquois clans were headed by chiefs, who would, as the occasion demanded, come together in council to govern their village and tribe. Tribal councils, in turn, chose representatives to the council of the Five Nations League itself. At every level such leaders were men, but women were not entirely left out; on the contrary, their role was critical. For one thing, local chiefs were selected by clan matrons (elder women).

Typically, when a chief died, the matrons would review the ranks of adult clansmen and then nominate a successor. Moreover, the matrons met more or less regularly to discuss policy; their opinions, as conveyed subsequently to the chiefs, carried much weight.

Even in warfare, apparently the prime responsibility of men, women played an important part. Some Iroquois wars were fought to avenge wrongs done to an individual or a family; others were "mourning wars" designed to secure captives who might replace and "requicken" (bring back to life) deceased members of local clans.

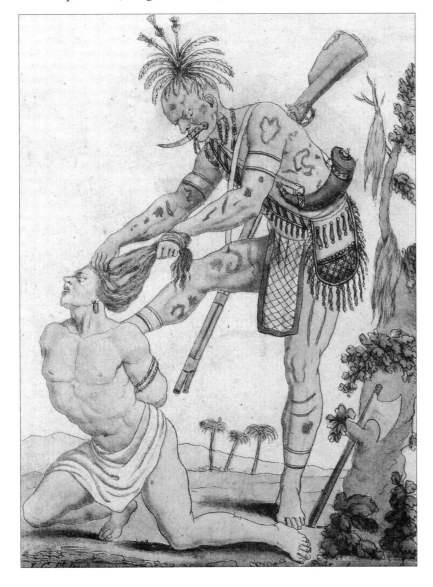

A 1787 French engraving of an Iroquois warrior scalping another Indian. Although war was an activity dominated by men, Iroquois matrons did participate in deciding who to fight and when.

Chiefs of the Iroquois Confederacy gather for a meeting in this 1724 engraving. Government and diplomacy were considered part of the "forest world," the realm controlled by men.

Either way, the wishes of women, especially the matrons, would likely prove decisive. One whose husband or son had died in battle could virtually require her kinsmen to start a mourning war. And when the battle was over, the same woman might decide the fate of any captives—whether to "send them to the flames" (a common European description of ritual torture and execution by burning) or to adopt them into her own or another village family. Women participated even in the torture process itself. They were part of the gauntlets (armed groups arranged in a line) of aroused villagers who taunted and beat newly arrived captives. And they were also in the crowds that carried out decrees of full-scale immolation.

The total of rights and duties assigned to women has long impressed observers from outside the country of the Iroquois. Some early visitors, noting especially women's work obligations, reduced it all to "enslavement"—Iroquois women as slaves to their husbands. But others reached the opposite conclusion. According to a missionary at the beginning of the 18th century, "it is they [the women] who really maintain the tribe... In them resides all the real author-ity." Modern anthropologists and historians are inclined to side with the second viewpoint; many go so far as to use the term *matriarchy,* meaning a society in which women rule. The Iroquois matrons, writes one historian, had more prestige and power "than women have en-joyed anywhere [else] at any time."

Longer than most Indian groups—perhaps longer than any—the Iroquois managed to hold their space against the pressures of colonization. Their contact with Europeans began soon after the opening of the 17th century, and they were still a substantial pres-ence at the time of the American Revolution 150 years later. Indeed, at least a portion of their ancient tribal grounds has remained with their descendants right to the present day.

The first Europeans they saw were undoubtedly traders. By 1620 Iroquois were visiting a Dutch outpost called Fort Orange, on the site of present-day Albany, New York, to exchange furs for guns, cloth, liquor, and other European-made goods. This was, in fact, the start of a pattern that would greatly change their lives. From self-sufficient producers (and consumers of what they produced) they were transformed into vigorous participants in the international market system. This, in turn, pulled them into increasingly complicated, often violent, relations with a variety of Indian and European neighbors.

In the 1620s the Mohawks fought and defeated the Mahicans to their east; this assured Iroquois dominance in trading with the Dutch. In the 1630s and 1640s Iroquois war parties began raiding Huron and Algonquin convoys to the north and thus intruded them-selves into the trade of French Canada. In 1649 a large Five Nations attack force overwhelmed and dispersed the Hurons and also de-feated a number of neighboring tribes in what is today Ontario. In the late 1650s they turned on the Eries (to the west), in the 1670s on the Susquehannocks (to the south), and in the 1680s on the Illinois (farther off toward the Great Lakes). Their motive in every case was economic: to control the Indian side of the ever-widening fur trade. Their success in these Beaver Wars would establish their superiority throughout the woodland regions of eastern North America.

Success also brought them more fully to grips with the Eu-ropean colonizers. The French opposed Iroquois moves against the tribes of Canada, many of which were French allies, and mounted

This treaty, signed in Montreal in 1701, established peace between the Iroquois and other Indian tribes allied with the French. The two rows of marks, at the bottom, are the signatures of the Native American chiefs.

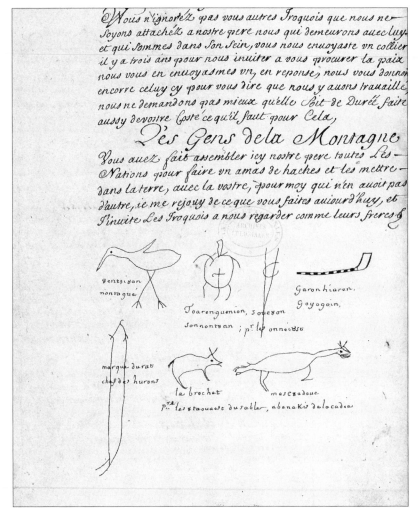

periodic invasions against the Mohawks, Oneidas, and Senecas. The Indians replied with sharp, bloody strikes of their own; by the 1690s French colonists at Montreal and other Canadian sites were living in daily fear for their lives. Fortunately for both sides, peace was finally achieved through elaborate treaty negotiations in 1701.

In spite of all their victories, the Iroquois suffered grievously from this century-long period of warfare. Young warriors died by the hundreds. (There were not more than a few thousand to begin with.) And to these losses "on the warpath" must be added the huge toll taken by recurrent epidemic disease. Village populations could be suddenly halved (or worse), and the overall number of Iroquois was in a steep decline. Each of the Five Nations tried to replenish its ranks by incorporating war captives, and in certain villages former captives actually became a majority. But this created new complications: villages were increasingly divided by differences of culture, language, and personal loyalty.

There were changes, too, in local power structures. The traditional chiefs seem gradually to have lost authority, and war leaders took their place. Moreover, because men were so frequently away at war, the village world was even more fully controlled by women. There is evidence that the power of the matrons increased and that the women's councils attained greater and more direct influence in matters of policy. Some 18th-century visitors to the Iroquois reported the presence of "she-sachems" (women chiefs), itself a new and significant development.

But there was more to the Iroquois experience of confronting colonization than trade and warfare. As with other native groups, religion proved an especially powerful factor. Dutch and English preachers paid at least occasional visits to the Iroquois throughout the period, but it was French Catholics based in Canada who made by far the greatest impact. The most active of these were Jesuits, members of a monastic order with worldwide plans and ambitions.

Jesuit missionaries were present in Iroquoia as early as the 1640s, and they remained even during periods of open French-Iroquois hostilities. Their eagerness to convert the "poor savages" was matched by their readiness to suffer and die for their faith; the combination was undeniably powerful. Jesuits penetrated even the most remote and unfriendly of Iroquois villages; some would remain for years or decades, would learn the tribal languages and customs, and would endure the taunts—or worse abuse—of their hosts. A few paid the ultimate price of death by torture when native opinion turned fully against them. Through their sacrifice, they became martyrs in the eyes of their fellow churchmen.

From the Indian standpoint these visitors were altogether strange. The Iroquois called them "blackrobes," after their severe monkish clothing. Their beards and body hair also seemed peculiar, since Indian men had little of either, and much of their behavior appeared unnatural, if not absurd. Their status as bachelors and their renunciation of any sexual interest were especially baffling.

In traditional dress but praying to the Christian cross, these Native Americans have integrated some aspects of Catholicism into their life. Although many Iroquois did respond to the message of Christianity, they often continued native religious practices as well.

Moreover, their difficulty in meeting the challenges of survival in the wilderness sometimes verged on the laughable.

For all that, Indians could not fail to notice the Jesuits' tenacity—or to listen, at least occasionally, to their message. They controlled a remarkable technology—including clocks, medicines, iron tools, and housewares, all of which were openly displayed in their residences. They displayed as well extraordinary powers of communication and memory through scribbled marks on parchment paper (their reading and writing). And their connections to "white chiefs," officials of the colonial governments, could yield valuable gains for the natives—trade preferences, for instance.

These factors weighed on the side of accommodating the missionaries. And many Iroquois went well beyond accommodation. With so much turmoil and violence around them, and with their own shamans (spiritual leaders) apparently unable to reverse the trend, some would decide to accept the Christian god. These converts might then become foes of others among their kin and neighbors who remained true to the old tribal beliefs. As an overall result, Iroquois villages became increasingly divided within themselves, with traditionalists on one side and newly declared Christians on the other.

As this conflict worsened, a growing number of the Christian villagers decided to leave. The Jesuits were starting mission communities for Indian converts in various parts of Canada, and the Iroquois were among the first to respond. These places would, with the passage of time, develop a strikingly mixed cultural pattern: they were Catholic in religion, but they also preserved many aspects of native tradition. The dwellings were likely to be longhouses. The diet was still centered on the "three sisters," especially corn. The women kept their old roles as farmers and gatherers, while the men continued to hunt and, when the occasion required, go off to war. Indeed, the paired worlds of village and forest remained largely intact.

The Jesuits, however, were not content to leave Indian life as it was, and they struggled for generations to effect change. Sex, marriage, and divorce were particular points of concern. Traditional Iroquois courtship practice was notably free, by Christian standards; sexual contact was generally allowed, or even expected. Out-of-wedlock births were, accordingly, quite numerous, and were accepted without stigma.

Marriage making was another matter; there the matrons took charge. The interests of the families were carefully weighed before a particular match could win approval. Divorce, on the other hand, was common, and was easily and informally managed; and there

Jesuit missionaries traveled throughout Iroquois country, determined to convert Indians to Christianity. Although they frequently lived and worked among the Indians for years, missionaries were sometimes attacked by "traditionalist" opponents. Here, Iroquois ransack a mission village in 1649 and torture the Jesuits.

was no bar whatsoever to remarriage. The Jesuits opposed these customs at every point. Courtship should, in their view, be closely supervised; the church, not the matrons, should oversee marriage; and remarriage should be entirely forbidden. The Indians gave lip service (at most) to the Jesuit position and quietly continued with their own ways.

The Iroquois response to Christianity itself was deeper and more complicated. The Jesuits insisted on teaching the essentials of the faith and claimed extraordinary success in doing so. The Canadian missions gained wide publicity for this; visitors from outside were reportedly moved to tears by the "sober conduct" and "pious disposition" of the converts.

Strikingly, too, the women responded with particular fervor. The Jesuits' writings on native villages are full of vivid stories of women converts gathered in prayerful "sodality" (companionship), or pleading with reluctant relatives (especially husbands) to accept the "true faith," or reproaching local shamans for their "devil worship," or destroying the liquor supplies that made their neighbors drunk. Some, indeed, endured "painful persecution" by other villagers who supported traditional ways. A few paid for their beliefs with life itself—"in the fires," as Jesuit accounts put it, of native torture ceremonies.

The same pattern of female leadership revealed itself in the missions to the north. Indeed, the largest of these—called Kahnawake, near Montreal—witnessed an outburst of female "devotion" that has remained legendary ever since. It began with the arrival around 1680 of a young Mohawk woman named Kateri Tekakwitha. Converted by Jesuits sometime previously in her home village, Kateri brought to Kahnawake a remarkably intense focus on religious matters. Almost immediately, she became the center of a kind of cult, in which she and other mission women literally tortured themselves for their faith. They beat each other with whips, walked naked in the winter cold, fasted for days at a time, refused to sleep, and recited rosaries till their voices went hoarse—all this in the name of an ever-deepening piety. The men of the community watched with mixed fascination and envy; the Jesuits moved from wonder and excitement to growing alarm.

Converted by the Jesuits when she was a young woman, Kateri Tekakwitha inspired other Native American women to embrace Catholicism through her own remarkable example of devotion and self-discipline. The Catholic church is now in the process of declaring her a saint.

Eventually, Kateri took sick and died, and the movement she led simmered down. However, she was remembered thereafter as a kind of martyr; visitors came to her grave—indeed they still come—to pray for her blessing. For some she worked apparent miracles. And the Catholic Church, in the 20th century, has begun the process of making her a saint.

One can only speculate on the reasons why women led the way in converting from their native religion to Christianity. But Iroquois women had always been leaders of a sort. And, besides, certain elements of Catholic Christianity may have seemed especially appeal-

This Mohawk cradleboard, with elaborate carved and painted decorations, was probably made around 1875. In rearing their children, Iroquois women continued to pass along their heritage and traditions even after the tribe had learned to live among whites and had adopted many white ways.

ing to female converts: the tradition of reverence for the Virgin Mary, the honor accorded to numerous female saints, and the various sisterhoods of nuns, some of which had spread to the European colonies in North America.

In fact, however, the piety of the Christian Iroquois was more than a simple matter of conversion. For even as they embraced their new faith, they infused it with elements distinctively their own. They decorated the churches with wampum beads, wore traditional ceremonial dress to Mass, and added native harmonies to familiar hymns and chants. They invented new rites of penance and thanksgiving, reflecting the pattern of Iroquois feasts. The practices of Kateri and her followers resembled native "vision quests," in which young Iroquois sought spiritual knowledge through self-denial and deprivation. The result of all these changes was a distinctly native brand of Catholicism. Its features can be seen even today in the churches of Indian communities in both New York State and Canada.

The American Revolution was a critical and ultimately devastating event in the history of the Iroquois. For the first time the nations themselves were divided: four sided with the British, two with the revolutionary patriots. The fighting flowed back and forth through the tribal heartlands, leaving death and destruction in its wake. The climax was a brutal campaign, led by the patriot general John Sullivan, to burn the towns and croplands of the Indians (especially the Seneca) who remained loyal to Great Britain. Its successful conclusion left thousands of Indians without the means to support themselves, and many died soon thereafter from starvation or disease.

The post-Revolution years were no kinder to the Iroquois. Through a series of treaties, the new United States government peeled away large chunks of their lands and forced them to accept the status of a conquered people. These legal actions were followed by renewed pressures from Christian missionaries—this time from Quakers and other Protestants. Once again the idea was to detach the natives from their traditional ways and move them toward modern "civilization." The process was furthered by changes in the environment, especially the disappearance of the woodlands. No longer could hunting, fishing, and gathering form any considerable part of the Iroquois' life-sustaining activities.

These changes struck especially hard at the position of Iroquois men, who were obliged now to transform themselves from hunters and warriors into farmers and day laborers. Many succumbed to despair or escaped into alcoholism. The position of women, by contrast, was less directly undermined. Their farming and traditional craft production could be continued under the new conditions. And women's role in the household, in the clan, and in local governance seems to have remained as strong as it had been before. Moreover, their responsibilities in child rearing made them guardians of traditional Iroquois ways for the future.

In the long run, of course, it was all Iroquois—female as well as male—who suffered from the changes around them. But, also in the long run, their culture, like many others in Native America, would survive in at least modified form. And to this process of survival Iroquois women made a persistent, vital contribution.

CHAPTER 4

FUR-TRADE WOMEN
AND THE MIDDLE GROUND

Among the many factors shaping relations between Indians and people of European descent, none was more important than a small, furry animal—the North American beaver. Demand for furs began growing, worldwide, by or before the year 1500. Furs could be used to make robes worn against the cold of winter, and above all, furs could be turned into warm hats. In the 16th century furs were obtained principally from Russia and surrounding regions; by the 17th century they were coming increasingly from America. The soft undercoat of the beaver was especially prized by European fur dealers, but other animals were also important—muskrats, martens, deer, moose, and even bears.

At first, these animals were taken near the little settlements along the Atlantic coast. However, the supply (especially of beaver) was soon exhausted, so the trade moved steadily west. In the 18th century it penetrated the heart of the continent, eventually reaching the Rocky Mountains and the great bays of central Canada. It made its greatest impact in the vast wilderness surrounding the Great Lakes. Among the tribes most powerfully affected were several native to that area, including the Ojibwas, Chipewyans, and Crees.

Because the fur trade was so profitable, people from various nations wished to control its European end. For many decades the

A Great Lakes Indian woman uses birch bark to build a canoe.

French led the way in this competition. The government of New France, their colony in what today is Canada, tried to organize and regulate all aspects of the trade. Indians from the west were encouraged to bring their goods to huge fairs (markets) held annually in the city of Montreal. These were boisterous events, with much feasting, drinking, and speechmaking, the exchange of gifts, and the renewal of political alliances.

After the 1670s, however, the trade fairs declined in importance. Increasingly, furs were exchanged in the "Indian country" itself, through individuals on both sides. French traders journeyed alone or in small groups to native villages and hunting camps deep in the forest. Meanwhile, too, Englishmen tried to enlarge their own part of the trade. Then, in the 1750s and 1760s, the English defeated the French in a bitter war for control of North America, and the shape of the trade changed yet again. In the years

In this fanciful 1738 sketch by a visiting Frenchman, Canadian trappers shoot at humanlike beavers huddled around a tree. The profitable fur trade transformed life for the Indians of the Great Lakes region.

to follow, it was managed largely by huge corporations like the Hudson's Bay and Northwest Companies. Moreover, in the 19th century, English operations moved gradually from transporting and selling furs into trapping the animals in their native habitats.

Throughout this long sequence, the fur trade drew Indians and Euro-Americans closer and closer together. Wherever the trade was centered, there developed a kind of middle ground—a region where cultures met, customs clashed, life styles merged and blended one into another. Indians adopted certain "white" ways (clothes, for example, and food, and weaponry), while whites, for their part, adjusted to the ways of the natives. "Nous sommes tous sauvages" ("We are all savages"), wrote one French trader about his experience of the middle ground in the late 18th century.

Often, in fact, relations between the two sides passed through the stage of familiarity to real intimacy. There were few white women in the region of the middle ground, so traders would frequently set up with native "squaws." (This term, extremely common in previous centuries, now seems painfully racist.) Some of these relationships were actual marriages, formalized in church and at law; others were informal but nonetheless deep and long lasting; still others were affairs of a single season. But whatever their depth and duration, they helped to anchor a widespread pattern of interracial exchange.

Companionship for the traders, and sexual favors, were only the start of women's involvement in the fur trade; from these flowed a variety of related contributions—all of them indispensable.

Sturdy footwear was key to success in the trade—and survival in the wilderness: moccasins in summer, snowshoes in winter. And everywhere these were made by Indian women. The process was laborious, involving, for moccasins, the tanning, cutting, and shaping of animal hides, and, for snowshoes, the preparation and webbing of "sinews" (leather strands) to be stretched within a wooden frame. On one apparently typical expedition in the 1780s, according to the leader's account, the Indian wives of two French traders were kept "continually employed making shoes [moccasins] of moose skin, as a pair does not last... above one day." At about the same time a Scotsman trading on his own in winter lamented his lack of snowshoes: "I do not know what to do without these articles—see what it is to have no wives!"

As European traders and Indian trappers worked together, their customs and cultures mingled. At top, an Ojibwa woman wears a western jacket and ruffled-collar shirt with Indian leggings and moccasins; at bottom, in contrast, another Ojibwa wears native clothes and carries her child in a traditional cradleboard.

A reliable food supply was no less essential; here, too, Indian women made the key contributions. Some, for example, set snares to catch small game for the table; "my woman brings home 8 hares and 14 partridges," wrote an English trader with evident satisfaction in the summer of 1815. Others fished the wilderness rivers and dried their catch to preserve it for the future. Still others harvested wild rice from shoreline marshes. In springtime they took sap for sugaring from maple trees, and in summer they gathered berries from the forest floor.

But the most important food of all, in the middle ground, was Indian pemmican. And Indian women were its sole producers. Starting with fresh buffalo carcasses, they cut out a supply of stripped meat, dried it in the sun or over a fire, pounded it with mortars, added melted fat, and stuffed the finished product into sacks of animal hide, which were also of their own making. Thus prepared and packaged, pemmican could be transported far and wide; the fact that it was highly nutritious and kept well only added to its value.

In this 1850 drawing, Ojibwa women harvest wild rice in Wisconsin. The labor of Indian women was crucial in providing a reliable food supply for trappers and traders.

From all these activities of the women the traders derived a varied and usually ample diet. Occasionally, however, there were shortages or other situations of special need. One trader described a time when he was injured and without food "till the berries became ripe and the kind hearted Indian women brought me plenty." Another remembered how his Indian wife saved a large group from starvation because she alone possessed the skills of making and mending fish nets.

Besides performing such traditional domestic tasks—traditional in their own cultures as well as in that of the Europeans—Indian women contributed directly to the operations of the trade. Of obvious importance was their knowledge and skill in dressing (cleaning, cutting) furs; officials of one English company described how they "clean and put into a state of preservation all beaver and otter skins brought... undried and in bad condition." They participated, too, in making the canoes on which travel and transport so largely depended. In many native communities the women were carefully trained to prepare special tree roots called *wattape* for

Ojibwa women collect sap from maple trees. They would later boil it into sugar and use it to flavor their food.

sewing the seams of these craft. They also gathered gum for use in caulking, and fashioned canoe sails. Moreover, when the canoes were ready for the water, Indian women sometimes took a turn at paddling. A trader, returning home from a long wilderness trek, reported encountering three heavily loaded canoes, each one paddled by an English man and an Indian woman—the latter in the steering position.

Indeed, it was clear to all how much the trade depended on the labor of these women. A wilderness guide summed it up in the early 1770s. Women, he noted, were essential as porters (carriers of skins and supplies). Moreover, they "pitch our tents, make and mend our clothing, keep us warm at night; and, in fact, there is no such thing as travelling any considerable distance, or for any length of time, in this country without their assistance."

But even this does not exhaust the list of their contributions. Frequently, Indian women put their knowledge of the wilderness to direct use by serving the traders as guides. In addition, they could play the role of interpreters, or even of language teachers, for the men. In some cases, rival trading posts competed for the allegiance of women whose language skills were especially strong.

Finally, Indian women served, on several levels, as diplomatic agents for the traders. Often this process was entirely informal, but still highly important. Traders would need introductions to local chiefs and clan groups, which their native wives could readily supply. In fact, there were numerous occasions when female partners helped to smooth the way by furnishing contacts, delivering messages, resolving differences and misunderstandings.

Occasionally, their diplomacy rose to higher, more official

A model of an Ojibwa canoe. Women directly contributed to the success of the fur trade by helping construct canoes; they also paddled and steered the finished craft.

levels; a Chipewyan woman named Thanadelthur provides a good example. In 1713 Thanadelthur had been captured by Crees, who were traditional enemies of her own tribe. A year later she escaped and, though almost starved, somehow made her way to an English trading post. There she offered her services as a guide along the route to her Chipewyan homeland, and the English governor, anxious to extend the range of his trade, quickly took her on. In the long expedition that followed, Thanadelthur became very much a leader. Whenever disaster threatened, in the form of sickness, starvation, or enemy attack, she kept the group moving forward. When the route itself proved difficult, she set off alone and after many days of perilous travel reached her objective. When the Chipewyans and Crees seemed unwilling to trust each other, the Scottish trader William Stuart reported, "she made them all stand in fear of her; she scolded at some... and forced them to the peace." And when, at length, the expedition had returned home, the English governor acknowledged Thanadelthur's part as "the chief promoter and acter" in it.

Thanadelthur spent the next months advising on new possibilities for trade, and was about to lead another wilderness journey when she was struck down by illness. The governor tried frantically to nurse her back to health; when she died in spite of his best efforts, he "felt almost ready to break my heart." She had been, he wrote to his superiors, a person of "a very high spirit and of the foremost resolution that I ever see." Her loss, therefore, would be "very prejudicial to the company's interest."

Finally, some Indian women became direct participants in the trade, especially with small animals like rabbits and martens. After all, as one English visitor noted, in many tribes "the snaring and trapping [of small animals]... are the business of women," and their skills in such work were readily transferable to dealings with outsiders. A further step might lead them into direct partnership with European traders, where business, sex, and companionship were fully entwined.

It is important to understand all this from the viewpoint of the women involved. Why were they interested in forming such connections—with the trade, and with individual traders? And what were the consequences for their own lives?

The Reverend John West drew this depiction of a visit to an Indian camp in his journal, published in 1824. West was one of several Protestant missionaries who tried to persuade Great Lakes Indian women to abandon their "immoral" relations with white traders.

Often the traders made a poor first impression. Most Indians found European men physically unappealing—especially their facial and body hair. One group contrasted their own "soft and delicate" skin with the "ugly" appearance of whites. Another ridiculed the possibility of intermarriage, saying that "our [women] would not live with them, for they have hair all over their faces and we have none there or elsewhere." Moreover, Indians found Europeans to be rude in manner and personal style: impulsive, complaining, lacking in dignity and self-control.

Still, increasing familiarity would soften these impressions, at least for some. And other factors also worked, over time, to draw native women toward the traders. Christianity was one such factor. Missionaries noted that most of their converts were female; Indian men, after all, were frequently away on the hunt or at war, while the women were accessible on a regular basis at home. Once conversion had been achieved, a woman might prefer a Christian husband. Demography was a second and parallel factor: in some Indian communities women outnumbered men by large margins. Polygamy—having more than one wife at a time—could solve this problem, but not for women who had been Christianized. Indeed, the missionaries insisted with special vehemence on the principle of one man-one wife.

Most native women, of course, were not Christians, and most did not marry white husbands. Those who did make one or the other choice, or both, were unusual—and may well have been unusual to begin with. In fact, Indian cultures had long recognized special roles for certain women, roles that went against accepted tribal principles. There were, for example, a few who qualified as seers because of their ability to prophesy, and others who acted as healers of physical and psychological illnesses. Still others were known as "hunting women"; they accompanied men on the hunt, gave their labor as needed, and sometimes provided sexual favors as well. An additional group would actually go into battle with men as "warrior women."

All these women were exceptional; all violated the expectations that applied to others of their sex. But all were tolerated, and even to a degree admired, for their evident strength. And it does appear that women who married white men were similarly regarded. Perhaps some individuals in this last category had previously belonged to one of the others as well (for example, a hunting woman who became a trader's wife).

The very process of personal growth would sometimes forecast these outcomes. Indian girls, like Indian boys, would typically undertake a vision quest upon reaching the age of puberty. This meant a period of withdrawal from regular life, of fasting and intense prayer, and—if all went well—of dreams and visions about the future. Most girls dreamed of spirits who revealed the secrets of successful marriage, childbearing, and other aspects of domestic life. But future hunting women might dream instead of buffaloes and wilderness treks, while budding female warriors "saw" battles and weaponry. And the visions of at least one Indian girl predicted her marriage to a trader. As a European visitor to her village later wrote, "she dreamed continually of a white man, who approached her with a cup in his hand... She fasted for ten days... [and] when satisfied that she had obtained a guardian spirit in the white stranger who haunted her dreams she returned to her father's lodge." Her husband, some years later, would be a rich and influential Irish immigrant named John Johnston.

The father of the bride, himself an important chieftain, actually arranged this marriage, and other tribal leaders sought to encourage similar alliances. Indeed, women might themselves take the initiative in such matters. Colonial officials reported cases in which native women independently decided to "desert [their husbands] to live with the whites." One such case involved an Ojibwa chief's daughter who simply moved into a trader's house, and, as he himself later wrote, "the devil could not have got her out." The trader, having tried but failed to persuade her to leave, made her his "country wife" and fathered several children by her.

Such cases suggest that Indian women hoped to change their life situation through connections to white men. And some, no doubt, succeeded. Those who married resident traders and became themselves resident in one or another trading post had a comfortably domestic routine. No longer were they obliged to follow their clan or tribal group in a seasonal round of migration; no more would they have to serve as carriers of heavy loads. Indeed, in some cases their experience reversed traditional patterns; the wives of company

The Indian family of an employee of the Hudson's Bay Company in 1882. By this time, interracial households were common in the fur-trade country.

officials, for instance, would receive the service of others instead of offering it to family members.

Even women of humbler status were said by the traders to enjoy "a comparatively easy and free life" when attached to one of the trading posts. As producers of moccasins, snowshoes, and fishing nets, they achieved both recognition and respect. Their efforts in cooking, meanwhile, or in other aspects of housekeeping, benefited from the white man's technology. Metal pots were more versatile than bark containers, and ready-made cloth of cotton or wool saved the long hours previously spent in preparing animal skins. "Show them an awl or a strong needle," wrote one trader, "and they will gladly give the finest beaver or wolf skin they have to purchase it." Clearly, too, these women enjoyed the European garments and jewelry that were sometimes lavished on them. Traders took it as a matter of pride that their wives should make a fine appearance; hence their orders to company supply stores would often include shawls, scarves, garters, stockings, and other items of stylish feminine apparel.

Fur-trade women might also escape restrictions that would have applied to them in their native settings. Indians in the Great Lakes area, for example, had traditionally reserved choice foods, especially certain animal parts, for men; a woman who consumed these was considered likely to die. But, as one English observer wryly noted, "women living with the white men eat of... [the] forbidden morsels... without the least inconvenience."

Some visitors to the middle ground felt that native women exercised "unnatural" influence over their trader-husbands—indeed "that they give the law to their lords." A Chipewyan woman named Madame Lamallice seems a clear case in point. Married in the early 1800s to an officer of the Hudson's Bay Company, she nonetheless retained considerable standing with nearby Indians. Because she was a skilled interpreter and thus essential to company operations, her demands for special favors could not be refused. Eventually, she began a private trade in furs and other goods. And when her white competitors tried to stop her, she threatened to turn all the natives against them.

The maneuvers of Madame Lamallice reveal how Indian women, linked to white traders, might benefit from their position between cultures. In other cases their influence was directed against the natives on behalf of the traders. The Chipewyan Thanadelthur was especially active in protecting fair conditions of exchange. An English official described a time when Thanadelthur observed an Indian offering furs of inferior quality and "ketch'd him by the nose, push'd him backwards, and call'd him fool, and told him if they brought any [goods] but such as they were directed [to bring] they would not be traded." No Indian woman could have acted so force-fully toward a man in her own village or clan.

To be sure, Madame Lamallice and Thanadelthur may represent extreme cases of Indian womanpower. Other women, in different situations and with different men, fared much less well. Some were treated callously, even brutally, by their white partners; some were abandoned far from home; some were actually sold, like slaves, from one trader to another. In a few instances, Indian kinsmen of women thus victimized would attack—and even murder—the perpetrators in revenge. Around the year 1800 an Ojibwa chief spoke bitterly of the entire situation: "The whites...take [Indian] women not for wives—but to use them as sluts—to satisfy their animal lust, and when they are satiated, they cast them off, and another one takes her for the same purpose, and by & by casts her off again, and so she will go on...soiled by everyone who chooses to use her."

These, too, were extreme cases. For most native women connection to white traders brought a mix of losses and gains: material comfort along with isolation from blood kin; greater independence along with at least occasional insecurity and self-doubt. In some respects the health of trader-wives may actually have declined. They were, for example, more fully exposed to contagious diseases carried by whites—and also to the white man's "firewater" (alcoholic drinks). They seem to have been more frequently pregnant than women who remained in tribal settings, which meant an increased risk of illness and of death in childbirth.

Moreover, there were unavoidable strains in mixed-race households. Most Indian groups in the middle ground regarded the matter of child rearing as a woman's responsibility. But whites took a different line; in their view, a father should act as his family's leader. From this difference flowed recurrent conflicts of authority. Some white fathers wished to send their children away to boarding school, an idea that native mothers could neither accept nor understand. On the other hand, certain Indian practices, such as flattening the backs of infants' heads, met with strong objections from the fathers.

There is a final irony about the outcome of these unions: the women involved would eventually be displaced by their own children and grandchildren. Members of these younger generations, commonly known as *métis* (French for "cross-breed"), were an ever-growing presence in the middle ground. And, in the 19th century, it was largely to métis women that traders would turn for both personal and business partnership.

Such women were especially well-attuned to the demands of life between cultures. From their mothers they learned the skills needed for effective participation in the trade. Their needlework, for example, helped clothe the traders, and they continued the tradition of making wilderness footwear. At the same time, they contributed in

Flattening the backs of infants' heads was one native tradition that white fathers objected to. Mixed-race couples often had to modify their customs to achieve a harmonious household.

more European ways: by washing and cleaning, and by tending small gardens of fruits, herbs, and vegetables in the vicinity of the major trading posts. An English official in one such place commented that "the women here work very hard; if it was not so, I do not know how we could get on with the company work."

Some métis women were fluent in several languages, both European and Indian; hence they were particularly useful as interpreters. And their knowledge of native customs enabled them also to act as intermediaries between cultures, again following the pattern of their mothers. Meanwhile, however, their fathers tried to acquaint them with at least the basics of European culture. Schools appeared in the middle ground during the early 1800s; there métis children learned reading, writing, and the principles of Christian "virtue." Churches were also a powerful influence, and most métis were intensely Catholic. Thus educated and "civilized" (from the white point of view), these "daughters of the country" became all the more attractive to European men arriving from overseas. Indeed, marriage between traders and métis women became increasingly "the vogue," as one visitor put it, and in some cases served to strengthen ties within fur-trade society itself. A young trader, for example, might wed the métis daughter of his company boss and thus improve not only his personal situation but also his prospects of professional advancement.

The middle ground, with its strikingly bicultural way of living, lasted well into the 19th century. But eventually it, too, would succumb to new forces of social and economic change—above all, the coming of agriculture to replace fur trading, and then the coming of industry to replace agriculture. Farmers took wives from among their own people and brought them to settle. Thus, for the first time ever, the population of the Great Lakes country began to include significant numbers of white women. As this happened, native and métis partners seemed less and less desirable to white men; indeed, a white wife became a kind of status symbol.

By 1900 the forest was gone, the animals were gone, the fur trade was gone—and so too was the middle ground. The remnants of the original tribes were shunted onto small reservations, where they maintained their traditions as best they could. The métis, for

This sketch shows a Swiss colonist (center) at a Canadian settlement with his wife and children. By the end of the 19th century, as trapping gave way to farming, more and more white settlers took their families out west with them.

their part, went in one of two directions. Some gravitated with their Indian kin to the reservations; others, especially those who had been "whitened" by two or more generations of intermarriage, became fully absorbed into mainstream society.

But the extraordinary story of their predecessors—including those whom one historian has called the "women in between"—would be remembered to the present day and beyond.

CHAPTER 5

CHEROKEE WOMEN AND THE TRAIL OF TEARS

Throughout the region that is now the southeastern United States, and well up into the Middle West, the landscape is dotted with earth mounds of varying size and shape. Some are as tall as 100 feet, and six times that broad. Many are roughly pyramidal in form, though flattened on top. A few are quite irregular and elaborate and seem to represent the bodies of animals. All were made long ago, well before the first colonists arrived from overseas.

Until quite recently it was believed that the actual Mound Builders had also come, many centuries earlier, from overseas and had subsequently vanished, perhaps when overwhelmed by "savage" Indians. It was not believed that native peoples could by their own efforts have created such massively imposing structures. Yet we now know that the mounds were indeed built by ancient Indians, including the ancestors of the group known today as Cherokees.

In 1534 a Spanish explorer, Hernando de Soto, became the first European to visit the Cherokees in their highland towns near the southern end of the Appalachian mountain chain. He admired their physical appearance, their pottery and basket making, and their skills in hunting. He also noted their use of mounds as sites for ceremonial temples and sometimes for burials.

An 1888 photograph of Walini', a Cherokee woman, taken on the Qualla Reservation in North Carolina.

The Cherokees of this early date were a people apparently at one with their environment. Their way of life combined farming (which was performed entirely by women), hunting (done entirely by men), fishing, and intermittent rounds of gathering. Their towns were small, compact, and largely self-sufficient. The people themselves seemed strikingly friendly, even gregarious; their activities, whether of work, play, politics, or religion, were typically done in a group. Harmony was their supreme social value; hence they always viewed the goals of the community as more important than the interests of individuals.

Within this social system women were strongly positioned. The basic family unit was the matrilineage, a line of kin based on mothers. Women owned important properties—housing, for example, and the fields they farmed—and, at death, passed these on to their own blood relatives. A married man usually lived with his wife's matrilineage. Some men were polygynous, but in most such cases the co-wives were sisters or cousins. Divorce was readily accepted, and easily obtained. In the aftermath of divorce, a woman regained the full support of her parents, brothers, and other maternal relatives.

These earthen mounds in Ohio were built by ancestors of later Indian groups like the Cherokees. The mounds zigzag to form the image of a serpent, perhaps to represent an ancient god or clan leader.

An artist's view of what a Cherokee town looked like around 1762. In warm weather, the Cherokees lived in wooden shelters, but during the colder months, they moved into the conical houses, which had a hearth in the center.

Women frequently resorted to abortion and infanticide (killing newborn infants) as a way of limiting family size. At the same time, their role as childbearers was honored everywhere; so too were their contributions as providers of food. Priests could be either male or female, and women took the lead in important annual festivals, such as the Green Corn Dance held at the start of the harvest. Town government was managed by a council in which all adults participated. Only men held positions as chiefs and elders, but women freely declared their own opinions. Indeed, a few so-called Beloved Women—older and presumably wiser than the rest—made key decisions about warfare and the treatment of captives.

Because the Cherokees lived well back from the coast, they were not at first much affected by the arrival of white colonists. But around the year 1700 their situation began to change. Like Indians everywhere, they were highly vulnerable to the unfamiliar diseases brought from Europe. And, also like other native groups, they were heavily drawn into international trade. Cherokee huntsmen had long sought deer and bear in limited quantities for local consumption. Now they killed the same animals on a very broad scale and offered the hides in trade at colonial seaports.

As the 18th century went along, the shape of Cherokee life was transformed by these and other factors. Warfare with neigh-

A 19th-century example of a Cherokee basket. As managers of the tribe's crops, Cherokee women also produced the baskets, vessels, and tools they needed in their work.

boring tribes (the Tuscaroras, the Shawnees, the Yuchi) increased as hunters moved farther and farther out in search of game. White settlers, moving up into the mountains from the east, increasingly clashed with passing Indians. Colonial leaders in Virginia and the Carolinas pressed for land near, or even within, the traditional borders of Cherokee territory; beginning in 1721, a series of official treaties transferred such land from native to white hands in chunks of hundreds and even thousands of square miles at a time.

In the second half of the century the Cherokees were caught up in the colonists' wars, with ultimately devastating results. Twice, in fact, they fought on the losing side: first with the French (in the French and Indian War, 1754–63), then with the English and colonists loyal to the Crown (in the American Revolution, 1776–83). Each time they paid a heavy price as invading armies swept into their towns from below, burning and pillaging at will. Defeat was followed by the loss of additional land, either through government-

The British presented this silver gorget, or ornamental collar, to the Cherokee chief Outacite in appreciation for his help in fighting the French. The engraving depicts the coat of arms of George III.

The American artist George Catlin, who traveled among various Indian tribes in the early 19th century, sketched these two Cherokee men.

to-government negotiation or from the continuing encroachments of individual frontiersmen.

In the meantime, the Cherokees were experiencing important changes inside their culture as well. Their economy, and even their day-to-day existence, was steadily reshaped by the fur trade. Because of European demand, many of their menfolk now did little else besides hunt. The women were also pulled into trade-related tasks: preparing and processing skins for the market. Women's work in farming was changed by the introduction of European tools (iron hoes and shovels, for example) and European fruits and vegetables (potatoes, apples, watermelons, peaches). Imported pots and hearth tools altered old ways of preparing food for the table, and machine-woven blankets replaced garments made from animal skins. As part of the same process, women's traditional craft skills—such as molding and firing clay pots, shaping bone into combs, needles, and other small tools, and weaving fiber mats—were gradually abandoned, then forgotten. Some Cherokees lamented these results, especially when they increased dependence on outsiders. Said one chief in the

1740s, "every necessary of life we must now have from the white people."

There were changes, too, in Cherokee political and social organization. Leaders of the English colonies wished to deal with leaders of similar stature among the natives. But the Cherokees had no chiefs beyond the level of individual towns, so the colonists selected one for the role of "emperor." Thus began a process of centralizing power within the tribe that would last far into the 19th century.

An important side effect of this process was a gradual lessening of women's role in governance. Town councils had been open to female participation, but the councils were steadily losing their former importance. And since contact with whites mainly involved trade and warfare, and those matters had traditionally concerned Cherokee men, women were left more or less on the sidelines.

This cooking pot, stamped with a pattern carved from wood, is from sometime after 1540. By the late 1700s, traditional skills—such as pottery making and weaving— had declined as the Cherokees came to depend on tools and goods imported from Europe.

Still they did not fall entirely silent. A certain Nancy Ward, Beloved Woman from the native town of Chota, appeared in 1785 at a treaty conference concluding Cherokee participation in the American Revolution. Describing herself as "a mother of warriors," she exhorted the delegates to create a firm basis for peace between her own people and the newly formed United States. Two years later another Cherokee woman wrote to Benjamin Franklin on the same subject. She had argued for peace at a recent assembly of tribal leaders, had filled peace pipes for the warriors, and had sent some of the same tobacco to the United States Congress. Her letter to Franklin urged him to "rightly consider that woman is the mother of All— and the Woman does not pull children out of Trees or Stumps nor out of old Logs, but out of their Bodies, so that [men] ought to mind what a woman says." These words reflected the ancient Cherokee belief that women's role as mothers gave them special authority in guarding the welfare of society as a whole.

Peace was not finally restored to the southern frontier until 1794, and for the Cherokees it came far too late. Their lands had been greatly reduced by repeated cessions—first to colonial, then to state and federal, governments. Moreover, the territory that remained open to them had been nearly emptied of game animals. Their population had also been reduced by the combined effects of warfare and disease. Dozens of their ancient towns lay devastated, with survivors scattered to new sites deeper in the mountains. Ordinary members of the group faced extreme difficulty in meeting their most basic needs for food and shelter, and the authority of their chiefs was increasingly in doubt. There were, as well, white populations on every side: Americans to the north and east, Spaniards to the south, French in the west. Many of these, especially the notorious American pioneers, were pressing relentlessly forward—with an eye to further transfers (or seizures) of tribal land.

Still, at this critical juncture, new opportunities were about to open up for the Cherokees. The policy of the federal government would give them a choice—and a chance—not previously available. The policy was, in a word, to "civilize" them—to detach them from their "savage" ways and transform them into solid "republican" citizens in order to permit their eventual absorption into the larger American nation. In the context of the times, this seemed a strik-

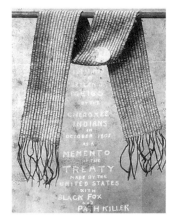

This Cherokee wampum belt commemorates a treaty with the U.S. government signed by Cherokee leaders Black Fox and Path Killer. The treaty gave up eastern lands in return for western territory. Repeated land cessions eventually forced the Cherokees off most of their traditional homeland.

ingly generous and enlightened prospect.

"The Indian," wrote President Thomas Jefferson, "is the equal of the European in mind and body." His cultural "backwardness" was but an accident of history; given a proper mix of encouragement and incentives, he would rise quickly to the level of whites. Jefferson pressed this viewpoint directly on Indians themselves. "You will find that our laws are good," he told a gathering of native leaders in 1808. "You will wish to live under them, you will unite yourselves with us, join in our great councils and form one people with us, and we shall all be Americans; you will mix with us by marriage, your blood will run in our veins, and will spread with us over this great continent."

The leading parts of the new policy included, besides intermarriage, education for native children, the conversion of as many Indians as possible to Christianity, and, above all, a shift in their economy to intensive horse-and-plow agriculture. What the latter meant specifically was that Indian men should abandon hunting and fur trading in order to learn farming, while their women became "homemakers" in a typical white-American sense. To enact this policy the federal government would offer plows, axes, seed, spinning wheels, looms, and other such implements to willing Indians. Missionaries would be encouraged to establish schools and churches in native communities. And the entire program would be supervised by resident government agents.

The program was intended for all Indians of whatever tribe; as events developed, however, the Cherokees would be its main focus. Nowhere else was the commitment of funds as large; nowhere else did hopes (especially among whites) rise so high. At first, in the early 1800s, Cherokee response was uncertain and divided. Some of the tribe seemed ready, even eager, to embrace the proposed changes. Interestingly, this was especially true of Cherokee women. A government agent described their "great earnestness [in]... the manufacturing of Cotton." Indeed, their interest was so great that "I have not been able to supply half the number who apply... for [spinning] wheels, [combing] cards, and looms, etc." The process may even have unsettled relations between the sexes. Cherokee men, reluctant as they often were to give up their status as hunters for that of farmers, probably shared the view of a chieftain among the nearby Creeks:

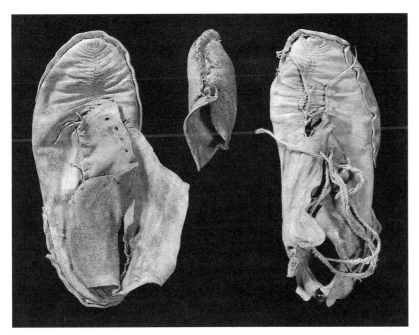

Using needles made of bone and deer sinews as thread, Cherokee women constructed these deerskin moccasins.

"If the women can clothe themselves," he said, "they will be proud and not obedient to their husbands."

Many Cherokees, women as well as men, resisted all pressures to change; for them tribal traditions remained strong. They believed, wrote one federal agent, "that they are not derived from the same stock as whites, and that the great spirit... never intended they should live the laborious lives of whites." Some defended old ways within their home villages, while others chose the path of escape. Thus some Cherokees began leaving for new destinations far to the west.

Meanwhile, the tribe was under constant pressure to yield additional lands. White frontiersmen were forever pushing forward, contesting native ownership, and, not infrequently, initiating or provoking violence. These people did not share the attitude of national leaders like Jefferson. To them the Indian was a racial inferior, a "red nigger" who was "radically different from all other men" (as newspaper accounts put it). Moreover, they believed, in the words of a frontier minister, that "his difference presents an insurmountable barrier to his civilization." They wished to see the natives "removed...as quickly and completely as possible."

The resident federal agents tried to steer a course midway between these extremes. Periodically, they would act to suppress violence and to chase the frontiersmen out. However, they also pressured the Indians to negotiate territorial transfers, especially of the old hunting grounds, for which, supposedly, there would be no further need. In fact, the agents secured the signing of seven more land treaties between the years 1800 and 1820. Each time Cherokee opinions were divided, with some in favor and others bitterly opposed.

Among the opponents were many Cherokee women. In 1817 a special women's council addressed the chiefs and warriors of the tribe in the following terms: "We have raised all of you on the land which we now have.... We know that our country has once been extensive, but by repeated sales has become circumscribed to a small tract.... Your mothers and sisters ask and beg of you not to part with

These Cherokee women were photographed in 1888 on the Qualla Reservation in North Carolina. They are making traditional pottery.

any more of our lands." A year later, when the chiefs were considering a plan to allot tribal lands to individuals, the women responded again. "The land," they declared, "was given to us by the Great Spirit above as our common right, to raise our children upon and to make support for our rising generations... We therefore unanimously join in our meeting to hold our country in common as hitherto." Holding land in common had meant, in practice, ownership by the matrilineal family. Thus a new system of individual ownership might significantly reduce the status of Cherokee women, since government agents, like most white Americans, saw men as the heads of families and owners of property. Land granted to "individuals" usually went to men.

Torn by internal divisions, and with their territorial base steadily eroding, the Cherokees seemed at this point to be set on a course of extinction. But after about 1820 they entered a new, remarkable, and much more promising period of their history—what one historian has termed a "renascence." They achieved, in the first place, a unified stance against further loss of their lands. And they also began, as never before, to accept the changes proposed by the United States government.

For example, they took up farming on a broad scale. Some, indeed, followed their white neighbors of the "Old South" in adopting a plantation model—including the use of black slaves and the intensive cultivation of market crops such as cotton. At the same time, increasing numbers of Cherokees embraced Christian religious beliefs and practices; a few became Protestant ministers. Schooling expanded, literacy broadened. And, in a particularly remarkable achievement, a Cherokee "mixed blood" named Sequoyah succeeded in reducing the tribal language to written form. This led, in turn, to a Cherokee translation of the Bible—and to the first regularly published newspaper in any Indian language. Capping the entire sequence was a major restructuring of tribal government: the creation of an elected council (in two parts, like the U.S. Congress), an executive authority headed by a single chief (somewhat like the U.S. Presidency), and a carefully graded court system to administer the law. These changes were formalized in the Cherokee constitution of 1828, which was itself modeled on the U. S. Constitution, written 40 years earlier.

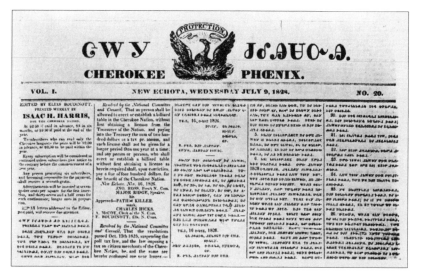

A Cherokee man named Sequoyah managed, in the 1820s, to devise an alphabet of 86 symbols (later reduced to 85) corresponding to the sounds of the Cherokee language. The front page of the Cherokee Phoenix *from July 9, 1828, has columns of both English and Cherokee text.*

Taken as a whole, the Cherokee renascence drew admiring notice from white citizens all across the country; "the most civilized tribe in America" was a comment frequently heard. But the effects were not evenly distributed. Wealth and other forms of personal benefit went disproportionately to a small group of highly assimilated Cherokees: men who embraced Christianity and the culture of nearby whites, and who, in some cases, took white wives. By contrast, those who resisted assimilation continued to lead marginal and increasingly impoverished lives.

The changes had an especially powerful impact on the position of women. As the old matrilineal clans lost importance, a woman could no longer rely on her brothers and other blood relatives as her ultimate source of security. Within the narrower confines of her immediate household she occupied a place subordinate to that of her "provider" husband. Her traditional control of family property was more and more in question; when Cherokee men emigrated to the west, for example, the wives and children they left behind would sometimes be evicted from family farmsteads.

Tribal law struggled to blend old values with new circumstances. On the one hand, it said that "the improvements and labor of our people by the mother's side" should remain "inviolate" for as long as a woman lived. On the other hand, the death of her husband would bring a division of property among their children and *his* "nearest kin." These apparent confusions might easily lead to court cases, in which Cherokee women would have to retain attorneys to guard their vital interests.

Other laws brought changes no less unsettling. Marriages had to be licensed by local authorities. And the traditional practices of abortion and infanticide were made into crimes. Even where the laws were designed to protect Cherokee women—against rape, for example—enforcement was difficult. Individuals who could not read or write, and who had no experience with courts and lawyers, were understandably hesitant to press their claims.

Finally, the continuing decline in women's political participation was sealed in the Cherokee constitution of 1828. The right to vote was restricted to "free male citizens"; moreover, "no person shall be eligible to a seat in the General Council but a free Cherokee male, who shall have attained the age of twenty-five." With this explicit bar to female officeholding the Cherokees went beyond even the United States Constitution—perhaps in backhanded recognition of their women's once powerful role.

Nevertheless, some Cherokee women managed to retain at least a part of their traditional status. Local census rolls continued to include a good many female heads-of-household. An obituary

The role of women in tribal life continued to decline as the Cherokees became "civilized" under the U.S. government's supervision. These women in North Carolina were photographed wearing traditional dress in the early 20th century; by that time, Cherokee women had been forced into the role of "housewives" and had lost much of their social and political influence.

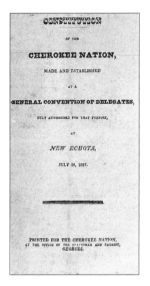

The Cherokee constitution, modeled on the U.S. Constitution, restricted voting rights and officeholding to males.

from the tribal newspaper in 1828 presents an especially striking case: a woman named Ou-dah-less, described as a major property holder and "the support of her large family." Other women were noted, well into the 1830s, as owners of slaves and proprietors of substantial plantations.

Whatever its short-term effects, the process of renascence was ultimately—and tragically—doomed. The demands of white settlers did not abate following the establishment of the new Cherokee government and constitution. Indeed, a policy of "removing" Indians gained official favor during the decade of the 1820s and was written into law by the United States Congress in 1830. The idea was that various native groups should trade their homelands for "open" territory beyond the edge of white settlement in the West. Some, such as the Creeks and Choctaws, readily accepted these terms, but the Cherokees did not.

Meanwhile, too, the state of Georgia was trying to extend its own authority over the Cherokee nation. The result was a series of lawsuits that went all the way to the U.S. Supreme Court. In 1831, Samuel Worcester, a white missionary, was arrested for residing among the Cherokees without a permit from the Georgia governor. Worcester appealed to the Supreme Court, claiming that the law he had violated was unconstitutional because it interfered with the sovereign status of the Cherokees. In 1832, the Court ruled in *Worcester* v. *Georgia* that the Cherokees were an independent nation, not subject to the laws of Georgia. Georgia officials, however, ignored the Court's decision, and the federal government refused to enforce it. Eventually, a small faction agreed to negotiate removal and in the Treaty of New Echota (1835) exchanged the tribal homeland for other territory in what is today the state of Oklahoma.

Most Cherokees rejected this agreement and vehemently refused to leave. But in 1838 federal leaders decided to evict them, by force if necessary. American soldiers proceeded, as a first step, to herd reluctant tribespeople into hastily built stockades. After weeks or months of virtual imprisonment, bands of Cherokee emigrants began to leave for the West. Facing unusually severe winter weather and lacking adequate supplies, they were very much at risk. Of the 15,000 who set out, at least 4,000 are believed to have died at one point or another along this "trail of tears."

The process of removal worked particular hardship on Cherokee women. According to the recollections of an army interpreter, many were simply "dragged from their homes by soldiers whose language they could not understand"; their children, meanwhile, "were often separated from them." In the stockades they were at the mercy of their white guards and "exposed to every species of moral desolation." A Methodist missionary reported the case of a "young married woman" who had been "caught" by soldiers, "dragged about," plied with liquor, and "seduced away, so that she is now an outcast even among her own relatives." According to the same source, "many [others] of the poor captive women are thus debauched through terror and seduction." The missionary did not use the word "rape," but that is clearly what he meant.

Once they were headed west, women continued to suffer. While a few (especially among the elderly) rode in wagons, most covered the entire 1,000-mile distance on foot. An eyewitness re-

The Trail of Tears (1840), a painting by Robert Lindneux, depicts the forced removal of the Cherokees from the Southeast to Indian Territory (in present-day Oklahoma). More than one-fourth of the people who began the journey perished en route.

In the early 1800s, before they were forced into the West, Cherokees typically lived in log cabins. This house was photographed much later, however. The woman at right is pounding corn in a mortar carved out of a tree trunk.

ported that many "were travelling with heavy burdens attached to the back." Some were pregnant and had to give birth by the trail. Others watched helplessly as their children took sick and died. And still others were themselves beset with mortal illness.

Those Cherokees who survived the "trail of tears" would find little comfort or compensation in their new homes in the West. A radically different environment of grasslands instead of mountain forests, another group of unfriendly white neighbors, plus the inherent difficulties in any such uprooting: separately and together, these factors would prolong the pains of removal for decades to come.

For Cherokee women in particular the process continued a long, downward spiral of change. The laws of their transplanted nation confirmed their exclusion from public life. The cultural values propounded by white missionaries, federal agents, and even their own menfolk stressed a narrow view of female "housewifery." There is evidence that they bore the brunt of increased personal violence

Officials of the U.S. government and white missionaries believed that Cherokee women should look and act like white women. Here, students at the Cherokee Female Seminary in Oklahoma in 1898 wear dresses and hats fashionable in white society. The school was modeled on Mount Holyoke Female Seminary (now called Mount Holyoke College) in Massachusetts.

when Cherokee husbands vented their own frustrations on other family members. As a leading historian of the Cherokees has recently written, "In the removal crisis of the 1830s men learned an important lesson about power; it was a lesson women had learned well before."

CHAPTER 6

INDIAN WOMEN CONFRONTING COLONIZATION

E ach of the numerous Indian cultures was different, in at least some ways, from all the others. And women's position within these cultures was also different. There were, however, similarities in the experience of such women, both before and after contact with foreigners. The Puebloans, the Iroquois, the Great Lakes tribes at the center of the developing fur trade, and the Cherokees: their separate stories of suffering and struggle, of accommodation and resistance and at least occasional triumph, reveal common threads that link the histories of Indian women everywhere.

The traditional patterns of Indian cultures almost invariably included a strong base in clan organization. Individual persons, both male and female, took their place in a group of relatives much larger than the nuclear family of parents and children. Typically, they married someone from outside the clan; but after marriage they remained close to their own blood kin.

In many tribes—the Iroquois and the Cherokees, for example—the clans were matrilineal; that is, property passed through the female line, from mothers to daughters to granddaughters. In some cases, the same was true of family names. (In such matters Indians differed greatly from Europeans, who typically transmitted both

A Hopi basket maker in 1901. Although most Indian groups were forced to adjust to white society and its demands, they also found ways to keep tribal traditions alive.

property and names through males.) Moreover, in some tribes—again the Iroquois and Cherokees are powerful examples—a married couple would usually live with the wife's relatives.

These patterns, taken as a whole, meant that women kept considerable power and influence through the link to their clan. For just as they remained loyal to the clan, so, too, did the clan remain loyal to them. When subject to abuse or exploitation, they were defended by their own blood relatives; if divorced from their husbands, they would be fully supported by the same relatives.

Marriage itself was begun and continued on roughly even terms. Young Indian women moved into and out of courtships as they pleased. In many native cultures sex before marriage was fully permissible; European travelers noted that Indian women had "free disposition over their own bodies." Divorce was also easily obtained— at the instance of either spouse (or of both).

Most Indian cultures expected women to play an important role as producers. Often they had the primary responsibility for farming: for planting, tending, and harvesting essential food crops. Typically,

Typically, Native Americans were organized into clans rather than nuclear families. Ojibwa wigwams, covered in birch bark and rush mats, would often house several generations of relatives, and even several families.

Ojibwa women braid rush mats around 1900. In most tribes, craft production remained women's work.

too, they were much involved with craft production (basketry, ceramics, and the like). Sometimes their skills extended even to house construction (the plastering done by Puebloan women) and to boat building (the work done by the Great Lakes women on canoes).

In all these activities women occupied a domain meant especially for their sex. Thus, for instance, the Iroquois defined an entire "village world" as belonging to women while reserving the "forest world" for men. These arrangements implied both separation and cooperation. Members of each sex were expected to contribute to the common good, and members of each would gain respect accordingly.

These attitudes applied also to spiritual life. Women were prominently featured in tribal myths and folklore. In some cultures women took the lead in important religious ceremonies (for example,

This 1657 engraving depicts a council of Indian men smoking ceremonial pipes. The chiefs of most tribes were male.

Concilium

the Green Corn festival of the Cherokees); in others they served as priests.

Governance, however, was principally in the hands of men. In a few cases women served as chiefs (the "she-sachems" of the 18th-century Iroquois), but in most the leaders were male. Still women did not lack influence. Often there were special women's councils to advise the chiefs on matters of policy. And on certain issues, such as starting wars, women might go beyond advising to actual decision making.

Behind this broad array of roles and duties lay a fundamental respect for women *as women*. Among most European peoples of the premodern era, to be female was to be considered inferior—a lesser version of the strong, wise, and more nearly "godlike" male. Indian cultures, in contrast, supported a balanced view of the sexes. Men were considered superior in some ways, women in others, and both were necessary to the survival of the group.

These, then, were leading themes in the experience of native women before their cultures entered into contact with Europeans. But the process of contact would vastly change them and their cultures. Some groups accommodated change quite readily; others resisted for longer or shorter periods; none escaped its effects indefinitely. Certain of the effects applied directly—and evenly—to both sexes. Disease, for example, struck down women and men in equal numbers. War, on the other hand, killed more men, since they were with rare exceptions the warrior group.

Over the long term, the combination of disease and war would so drastically reduce Indian populations that community life itself was reshaped. Villages might see their numbers cut in half within the space of a decade or a generation, and among the surviving group the ratio of women to men might be badly skewed. In one case for which there is particularly good evidence—the Iroquois village of

A 19th-century portrait of an Ojibwa widow. The bundle she holds is a collection of her husband's things that she has gathered and will keep with her for a year. Warfare among tribes and with Europeans killed many Indian men and devastated whole villages.

Kahnawake, near Montreal, in the 18th century—females outnumbered males by nearly three to one. It was in such extreme circumstances that the influence of women's councils might temporarily expand—and that some women would actually become chiefs. One imagines as well a powerful effect on family life: more and more widows, fewer and fewer potential husbands, numerous children growing up without fathers.

Trade was another focus of change in the lives of Native Americans. And here, too, the process affected men and women in different ways. Typically, men were the leaders in trade, partly because men were the hunters (and animal furs were sought, above all else, by whites) and partly because whites preferred to deal with men in these matters. Women, by contrast, performed support roles: preparing goods for the market, carrying them to trading sites, and supplying the men with food and other necessities of everyday life. In contrast to the balance of their native cultures, women came to occupy a secondary place, distinctly behind that of men, in the economies of trade-focused tribes.

Trade also served to undermine various forms of traditional craft production in which female participation had once been central. Fewer and fewer women would now earn status and influence by making fine baskets or pots or jewelry; instead, such articles (or their European equivalents) were imported from outside the community. Moreover, the activities they supported also moved away from traditional patterns. Food preparation, for example, was transformed by the use of iron cookware, while native diet was altered by previously unknown foodstuffs (vegetables and fruits introduced from overseas).

These changes were most evident in situations where Indians encountered whites on a group-to-group basis. But clearly, too, there were other situations in which individual encounters took precedence. Wherever the newly arriving white population was predominantly male, Indian females became a focus of interest and sometimes of coercion. This was especially true in the case of fur traders, who actively sought native women as sexual partners, as helpers and collaborators in work, or simply as domestic companions.

In this 1724 French depiction, Native Americans have incorporated European clothing into their traditional dress. Trade with whites affected most areas of the Indians' life and often became a focus of their activities.

Some of these women were themselves eager for such connections; evidently they preferred the role of trader's partner to that of tribal spouse. A few managed to use their opportunities as a way of entering the trade on their own account. However, many others endured abuse, abandonment, and exploitation at the hands of their white partners. And often enough, for this latter group, there was no returning to their communities of origin; they remained thereafter apart from both white and native cultures.

Indian women also encountered other individuals (besides fur traders) from the white side. There were government agents, like those sent to the Cherokees to promote the federal policy of "civilization." And there were soldiers, like the ones assigned to enforce removal. These encounters would leave the women with decidedly mixed results. From the agents they received the "gifts" of a supposedly more advanced technology (such as looms, spinning wheels, and other implements of domestic production). But with the soldiers they experienced the brute power of an alien government—and sometimes, too, assaults on their very persons.

Along with the white man's government came the white man's churches; often, indeed, the churches arrived first. The friars in the Puebloan country of the Southwest and the Jesuits who sought out

Whites introduced Indian women to spinning wheels, looms, and other European technology that drastically changed the pace and nature of their work.

the Iroquois in the Northeast were just the vanguard of a centuries-long, continent-wide missionary project. In some cases this project achieved its earliest and strongest successes with Indian women. The women, after all, were more readily accessible, at home in their tribal villages, than the men. And the women could respond directly to key elements of the Christian system of worship: for example, the adoration of the Virgin Mary and the creation of numerous female saints in Catholicism.

The impact of these alliances—white missionaries with native women—was, however, finally disruptive of traditional culture. Christian converts would have to reject many of the beliefs and values with which they had been raised. And female converts in particular would have to adjust to a religious system in which the Deity Himself and His principal earthly advocates (priests and ministers) were all unmistakably male. Moreover, the same system identified a specific woman (Eve, in the Bible) as the "root of all evil" and attributed to every female born thereafter a share in the stain of her "original sin." The mission churches were, in short, little patriarchies.

There is no simple method for calculating the sum of these encounters, whether between groups or among individuals. But clearly, in many respects, Indians were obliged to give way. Every native culture brought closely to grips with encroaching whites would emerge—after decades or centuries—irrevocably transformed. Some, indeed, would entirely disappear. The power of such transformations can best be grasped through a process of before-and-after comparison: before the whites arrived, and after the effects of contact had been substantially worked out.

Family relationships, first of all, were pushed in the direction of European norms, as Indian households became more and more nuclear. Loyalties to the larger clan would not be abandoned entirely, but the primary bonds became the ones between husband and wife and between parents and children. From a woman's standpoint, this meant a significant narrowing of personal support. No longer could she count on her own parents, her uncles, her siblings and cousins to come automatically to her aid in times of need. Was her marriage proving difficult? She must try to make the best of it. Were her children failing to grow and learn as expected? She must find her own solutions. New living arrangements—separate, for the most part, from those of clan relatives—reinforced the trend. A wife's ties to her husband (and his to her) became the basis of all her experience.

Increasingly, too, these ties expressed a kind of inequality. Christian churches, schools run by whites, and U.S. government agencies all propounded an American model of marriage, with the husband serving as head and the wife as his "helpmeet." As part of the same model, men would take the role of providers while women would center their lives on home. This corresponded also to ongoing changes in native economies. Farming replaced hunting and trade as the major source of subsistence for many Indian groups. And farming became to an ever greater degree the work of men.

Obviously, these changes served to reduce the economic worth of women's labor. And, at the same time, women were losing their connection to property. The old matrilineal principles slowly but

A married and unmarried woman—her status indicated by the hair whorls—inside a Hopi house. As Indians adopted white ways, a woman's bond with her husband took precedence over the ties to her clan relatives.

steadily weakened. Under the new conditions men owned property and men controlled inheritance. In all this, Indians were pressured to follow the pattern—and the law—of whites, according to which married women had little or no standing of their own. Instead, they were seen as "covered" by the men closest to them, principally their husbands.

Women's part in governance also shrank—also in conformity to white standards. As the clan system lost influence, so, too, did the clans' leading women (the matrons of the Iroquois, for example). And the new systems adopted by Indians (such as the one embodied in the Cherokee constitution of 1828) would typically exclude women both from voting and from holding office. Like their white counterparts, Indian women were pushed to the political sidelines.

The events and trends described here express, beyond any doubt, a long-term process of decline. Indian women were *losing* opportunities, influence, and status that had formerly belonged to them. The process was not uniform either in its timing or in its specific details—and individual tribes were affected in at least somewhat different ways—but its direction was everywhere the same.

The decline for women was, of course, just a piece of the larger decline of Native Americans in general. Indian men lost out as well—and in some respects lost more directly, more painfully—in the unfolding encounter with peoples of European extraction.

And yet there is more to the story than this. Indians did not simply surrender; rather, they responded to their losses with courage, flexibility, and a sometimes extraordinary resourcefulness. The survivors of shattered tribes would regroup and join together to make a new stand against continuing white encroachment. Ancient tribal traditions—the customs, beliefs, and values at the core of their historical experience—would be carefully preserved for the future. Native cultures might bend this way or that, but seldom did they break. Even now these cultures live on, albeit under tightly constricted conditions and outside the notice of the American mainstream.

Women's part in these efforts to preserve Indian culture has been consistently important. In some cases (for example, the Cherokees in the early 19th century) native women struggled valiantly for the preservation of tribal lands. In others (the Iroquois, also in the 19th century) they anchored a process of strategic retreat. In others (the fur-trading tribes of the Upper Great Lakes) they helped to create a middle ground on which native people could try to hold their own, at least for a time. In still others (for example, the Puebloans, in the 20th century) they initiated a kind of cultural revival by recovering the craft traditions of remote ancestors. It is certain, too, that in the privacy of countless Indian households old cultural ways

In 1922, Ojibwa women use traditional skills to make birchbark containers for holding maple sap. Even in the face of 20th-century technology, Indian women have preserved their culture, in part by continuing the craft traditions of their ancestors.

were remembered and valued—and passed on, across the generations—by individual mothers and their children.

Considering, then, the full range of Native American experience, we cannot summarize these histories in terms only of decline. Adaptation, recovery, and survival—such words also apply. And the struggle continues still.

CHRONOLOGY

about 20,000–15,000 B.C.	First Indian people arrive in the Americas
about 5000 B.C.	Some Indians begin to practice farming
1000 B.C.–A.D. 1000	Rise and fall of major Indian civilizations (Olmecs, Mayas, Aztecs)
1492	Indians' contact with Europeans begins
about 1500	League of the Iroquois Five Nations is established
1539	Puebloan Indians are conquered by Spanish colonizers
about 1620	Fur trade begins between various Indian groups and European colonizers
about 1640	European missionaries begin efforts to convert Indians to Christianity
1680	Puebloans revolt against the Spanish but are reconquered soon afterward
1701	Iroquois and French make peace after many decades of war
1721	First of numerous treaties between Cherokees and colonial governments (and later the federal government) in which the Cherokees cede tribal lands
1776–83	The American Revolution brings great loss and suffering to various Indian groups, especially the Iroquois and the Cherokees
1760–1820	The center of the fur trade shifts west, from the coastal regions to the area of the Great Lakes
1820–30	Period of the Cherokee "renascence"
1838–40	Cherokees are removed to western land along the Trail of Tears

FURTHER READING

A Note on Sources

In the interest of readability, the volumes in this series include no discussion of historiography and no footnotes. As works of synthesis and overview, however, they are greatly indebted to the research and writing of other historians. The principal works drawn on in this volume are among the books listed below.

Anderson, Karen. *Chain Her by One Foot: The Subjugation of Native Women in Seventeenth-Century New France*. New York: Routledge, 1990.

Armitage, Susan, and Elizabeth Jameson, eds. *The Women's West*. Norman: University of Oklahoma Press, 1987.

Bataille, Gretchen M., and Kathleen M. Sands. *American Indian Women: A Guide to Research*. New York: Garland, 1991.

Devens, Carol. *Countering Colonization: Native American Women and the Great Lakes Missions, 1630–1900*. Berkeley: University of California Press, 1992.

Etienne, Mona, and Eleanor Leacock, eds. *Women and Colonization*. New York: Praeger, 1980.

Evans, Sara M. *Born for Liberty*. New York: The Free Press, 1989.

Graymont, Barbara. *The Iroquois*. New York: Chelsea House, 1988.

Green, Rayna. *Women in American Indian Society*. New York: Chelsea House, 1992.

Gutierrez, Ramon. *When Jesus Came, the Corn Mothers Went Away: Marriage, Sexuality, and Power in New Mexico, 1500–1846*. Stanford, Calif.: Stanford University Press, 1991.

Hornbeck-Tanner, Helen. *The Ojibwa*. New York: Chelsea House, 1992.

Jensen, Joan M., and Darlis A. Miller, eds. *New Mexico Women: Intercultural Perspectives*. Albuquerque: University of New Mexico Press, 1986.

Landes, Ruth. *Ojibwa Woman*. New York: Columbia University Press, 1938.

McLoughlin, William G. *After the Trail of Tears: The Cherokee's Struggle for Sovereignty, 1839–1880*. Chapel Hill: University of North Carolina Press, 1993.

———. *Cherokee Renascence in the New Republic*. Princeton, N.J.: Princeton University Press, 1986.

Namias, June. *White Captives: Gender and Ethnicity on the American Frontier*. Chapel Hill: University of North Carolina Press, 1993.

Nash, Gary B. *Red, White, and Black: The People of Early America*. Englewood Cliffs, N.J.: Prentice-Hall, 1974.

Niethammer, Carolyn. *The Lives and Legends of American Indian Women*. New York: Collier, 1977.

Perdue, Theda. *The Cherokee.* New York: Chelsea House, 1989.

———. "Cherokee Women and the Trail of Tears," *The Journal of Women's History* 1 (1989): 14-28.

———. *Slavery and the Evolution of Cherokee Society, 1540–1866.* Knoxville: University of Tennessee Press, 1979.

Quimby, George I. *Indian Life in the Upper Great Lakes.* Chicago: University of Chicago Press, 1960.

Richter, Daniel K. *The Ordeal of the Longhouse: The Peoples of the Iroquois League in the Era of European Colonization.* Chapel Hill: University of North Carolina Press, 1992.

Riley, Glenda. *Women and Indians on the Frontier, 1825–1915.* Albuquerque: University of New Mexico Press, 1988.

Schlissel, Lillian, Vicki L. Ruiz, and Janice Monk, eds. *Western Women: Their Land, Their Lives.* Albuquerque: University of New Mexico Press, 1988.

Seaver, James E. *A Narrative of the Life of Mrs. Mary Jemison.* Edited by June Namias. Norman: University of Oklahoma Press, 1992.

Shirley, David. *The Pueblo Indians.* New York: Chelsea House. 1994.

Shoemaker, Nancy. "The Rise or Fall of Iroquois Women," *The Journal of Women's History* 1 (1989): 39-57.

Van Kirk, Sylvia. *Many Tender Ties: Women in Fur-Trade Society in Western Canada.* Winnipeg, Canada: Watson & Dwyer, 1981.

White, Richard. *The Middle Ground: Indians, Empires, and Republics in the Great Lakes Region, 1650–1815.* New York: Cambridge University Press, 1991.

INDEX

Acknowledgments

The author wishes to acknowledge a special debt, in the course of preparing this book, to works (cited in the Further Reading) by the following authors: Ramon Gutierrez, William G. McLoughlin, Theda Perdue, Sylvia Van Kirk, and Richard White.

Picture Credits

John Demos is the Samuel Knight Professor of American History at Yale University. He is the author of several volumes of colonial history, including *The Unredeemed Captive: A Family Story from Early America,* which was nominated for the 1994 National Book Award; *A Little Commonwealth: Family Life in Plymouth Colony;* and *Entertaining Satan: Witchcraft and the Culture of Early New England,* for which he was awarded the 1982 Bancroft Prize in American History. He is also the author of *Past, Present, and Personal: The Family and the Life Course in American History.* Professor Demos has also received fellowships from the American Council of Learned Societies, the National Endowment for the Humanities, and the John Simon Guggenheim Foundation.

Nancy F. Cott is Stanley Woodward Professor of history and American studies at Yale University. She is the author of *The Bonds of Womanhood: "Woman's Sphere" in New England 1780–1835, The Grounding of Modern Feminism,* and *A Woman Making History: Mary Ritter Beard Through Her Letters;* editor of *Root of Bitterness: Documents of the Social History of Amercian Women;* and co-editor of *A Heritage of Her Own: Toward a New Social History of American Women.*